SPYING

THE SECRET HISTORY OF HISTORY

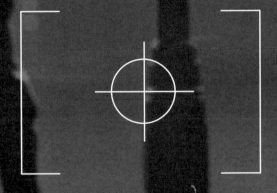

INTERNATIONAL SPY MUSEUM WITH DENIS COLLINS

BLACK DOG
& LEVENTHAL
PUBLISHERS
NEW YORK

INTERNATIONAL
SPY
MUSEUM

ACKNOWLEDGEMENTS

With special thanks to Kathleen Coakley, Vice President of
Exhibition Management for the International Spy Museum;
Peter Earnest, Executive Director of the International Spy Museum;
Thomas Boghardt, PhD., Historian; and Joan G. Stanley of
J. G. Stanley & Co., Inc.

Published by
Black Dog & Leventhal Publishers, Inc.
151 West 19th Street
New York, NY 10011

Distributed by
Workman Publishing Company
708 Broadway
New York, NY 10003

Manufactured in the United States of America

Cover design by Sheila Hart Design
Interior design by Edward Miller

Cover photograph courtesy of CORBIS.

ISBN: 1-57912-395-3

h g f e d c b a

Library of Congress Cataloging-in-Publication Data available on file.

CONTENTS

FOREWORD

In 2002 we opened the doors to the International Spy Museum in Washington, D.C., for the first time. It was July 19th, a typical mid-summer, sun-scorching day in the nation's capital, and it was the first such museum in the world. Would the public come? The answer would come in the days and weeks following that exciting first day opening ceremony which featured the city's mayor (in disguise no less!) and many well-known, former officials from Washington's intelligence community.

The answer arrived in the form of thousands of visitors of all ages: men and women, children and families, school groups and seniors, all of whom waited patiently in line for hours to enter. It would be weeks before we found a way to pace visitor arrivals and to eliminate the block-long lines. The International Spy Museum was an instant success. Eighteen months later, over one million visitors had passed through the doors. What brought them to the museum in such numbers?

There is no question: it is that craving in each of us to know the unknown, to get behind the scenes, to see, how things work. Don't we all have it? That's what draws the crowds. As executive director, I meet visitors every day who tell me that it is the mystery and intrigue of spying and how it's done that led them to visit the museum to see for themselves. There is a saying at the museum which is, "Now you'll know." That's what brings these many visitors to our doors. And that's why so many leave with a knowing smile.

Paging through *Spying*, you will see the world through a different lens, one that reveals the hidden story behind the events that you thought you understood—until now. These are stories of men and women who risked their lives and fortunes to change the course of history.

From time to time, their clandestine exploits are publicly revealed, sometimes by their own hand (or pen!) but more often by an enterprising author or the ever-vigilant press. Whatever the source, we soon realize that those who have chosen the shadow world can be found in the service of every nation and cause. Some hail them as heroes; others, as spies and traitors. Throughout history, such men and women will be found on all sides. No nation and no cause has a monopoly on dedication, courage, and cunning.

These are stories about the real world, of secrets exposed, and of the truth brought to light. In reading about the inner workings and hidden corridors of this shadow world, you will have gained new insight into the silent players who act behind the scenes and of how their exploits did indeed change history.

Now you, too, will know.

Peter Earnest
Executive Director, International Spy Museum
Washington, DC, 2004

INTRODUCTION

Major General David H. Petraeus of the U.S. 101st Airborne stood squinting into an Iraqi sandstorm, blind to Fedayeen irregulars, Republican Guard troops, and any other freelance unfriendlies who might be crawling his way with grenade launchers. His assault on Baghdad had ground to a precarious halt in what was supposed to be safe territory.

Now Petraeus, a division commander in the world's greatest army, turned to an embedded newspaper reporter and said, "The CIA really needs to pull one out."

Weeks later, as he led his troops into Baghdad after a nearly casualty-free assault, Petraeus's wish had been granted. While the rest of the world wondered at the lack of resistance outside the city, Petraeus could thank his country's Central Intelligence Agency for clearing his approach, not with sophisticated assault weapons or laser-guided bombs but the old-fashioned way—by putting operatives on the ground to bribe and blackmail enemy military commanders into abandoning the field. American intelligence would be faulted later, but on that patch of sand in that lethal time, the results were more than welcome.

The CIA's role in the taking of Baghdad may never make it into standard history textbooks. But few know that George Washington's Revolutionary army would most likely have quit its first winter at Valley Forge if not for the appearance there of an undercover agent—an Irishman chasing a cow; or that the Allied landings in Europe during World War II owed much of their success to some forged documents, rows of inflatable tanks, and a man who didn't exist. Those stories, like gnarled roots below the broader-leafed versions of famous events, reveal what might be called the secret history of history.

The "great man" interpretation of history credits powerful leaders for shaping world events, and although that certainly sounds nobler than the "defector with a shopping bag full of secrets" theory, each interpretation is at least half true. The biggest difference between them may be star billing—espionage agents and their operations aren't cast for center stage. Consider the Allied success in breaking Germany's Enigma code during World War II, a project that involved more than ten thousand people and saved countless lives. News of that tremendous achievement did become public—but not until 1974, a bit late for curtain calls.

Spy stories are more often leaked than written, and they star not just patriots but also traitors, double agents, moles, defectors, and saboteurs. That is what makes them irresistible, along with the cloak and dagger, the necktie cameras, and the great escapes. It also helps to know that many of the most exaggerated spy tales are essentially true.

"A hundred ounces of silver spent for information may save 10,000 spent on war. —Sun Tzu, fourth century BC, Chinese general, strategist and spymaster

1.

SPY BUSINESS

It didn't always take a thief. The first known intelligence report, written on a clay tablet four thousand years ago, spoke of a secret mission to watch fire signals coming from villages beside the Euphrates River. And when Moses sent his spies, one from each of the twelve tribes, to scout the Promised Land, he asked that they report only on whether the people there "be strong or weak, few or many . . . and whether they dwelt in tents or strongholds."

Today espionage agents are expected to collect more than the low-hanging fruit. They are charged with knowing the difference between information and intelligence and, occasionally, with undertaking covert actions based upon that intelligence.

Yet the astronomical advancements in collection methods today do not alter the fact that the reason for espionage is the same now as it was when Chinese spymaster Sun Tzu wrote his best seller *The Art of War* in the fourth century BC: to protect against the threat posed by adversaries or gain advantage over them. The rest is gadgetry.

One way to look at the evolution of espionage is to see it as a continuous game of action and reaction. The moment people started reading each other's mail, there arose a need for codes, ciphers, and invisible ink. That, in turn, meant a lot of work for good code breakers.

Alexander the Great always encouraged his soldiers to send messages home to their loved ones, messages he secretly read for signs of dissension. In 1590 French king Henri IV created a government department, the *Poste aux Lettres*, charged with the sole task of intercepting internal mail. Whatever the initial aim of the agency, it eventually degenerated into a means of supplying the king and his ministers with titillating details of the sexual adventures of French society.

"The trade of a spy is a very fine one. . . . Is it not in fact enjoying the excitements of a thief, while still retaining the character of an honest citizen?—*Honoré de Balzac, nineteenth-century French journalist and writer*

Each subsequent advance in information gathering, from the telegraph and photography to wireless, computers, and satellites, has brought with it a need for more analysts, computer technicians, information managers—in short, an ever-expanding bureaucracy. Only in the past hundred years, however, has the growth in information technologies ballooned.

The United States, for example, routinely shut down its intelligence organizations after each war and did not create a permanent central intelligence agency until 1947. Today the country has fifteen separate intelligence agencies, which spend an estimated $82 million every day of the year. It's difficult to know how many people are currently employed worldwide in intelligence since agencies in the business of keeping secrets rarely open their books.

History proves, however, that increases in manpower and collection capability do not necessarily make for more effective analysis. As we'll see later, more information invariably means more opportunity for any particular detail to be lost in the labyrinth.

Still, in the intelligence business failure is often rewarded with more manpower and money. If the Egyptian pharaoh Merenptah had had a few more agents, the argument goes, there might never have been an Exodus. And in the age of nuclear weapons, when one security lapse might lead to annihilation, the argument in favor of increasing intelligence capacity is difficult to rebut.

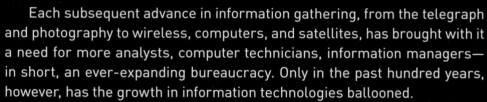

Spy Lingo

- **HUMINT:** Intelligence gathered by people.
- **TECHINT:** Technical intelligence.
- **SIGINT:** Signals intelligence.
- **COMINT:** Comunications intelligence.
- **ELINT:** Electronic signals intelligence.
- **PHOTOINT:** Photographic intelligence.
- **RUMINT:** Rumors intelligence.

The first large mail interception operation was undertaken by Austrian intelligence during the eighteenth century. Every morning sacks of mail to or from foreign embassies in Vienna were opened; the letters were copied, decoded if necessary, resealed, and sent on their way. Code breakers were given bonuses for solving difficult codes. The money came from profits the Austrians made selling the information to other European powers.

A message from Union Spy E. Van Lew, scrawled on a scrap of onionskin; opposite page: Invisible ink message written on the back of a female spy during World War I.

SPYMASTERS

The first spymasters were often prophets, soothsayers, or priests—educated men who not only recruited and trained agents but could also give them God's blessing for even the dirtiest work.

Cardinal Armand-Jean Richelieu, advisor and spymaster to the seventeenth century's King Louis XIII, served God and Louis with equal ruthlessness. He once said, "Give me six lines written by the most honest man, I will find something in them to hang him."

Cardinal Richelieu may have learned some of his cunning from Sir Francis Walsingham, spymaster for Queen Elizabeth I. In 1573, Walsingham inherited England's first secret service and then built it into a most formidable weapon to protect his Protestant queen from Europe's Catholic monarchs and their Jesuit advisers. He spent his own money to send agents to Europe and was rewarded with detailed plans for the forthcoming attack on England by the Spanish Armada. By undertaking the covert action of bribing Italian bankers to delay funding for the armada, Walsingham gave England time to prepare.

Perhaps the best of the twentieth-century spymasters was Feliks Dzerzhinsky, the son of a Polish nobleman who spent twelve years in a Russian prison before being put in charge of a pitifully small Russian intelligence organization (twenty-three agents) immediately after the 1917 Revolution. A quiet, courtly fellow with a fanatic love of Communism, Dzerzhinsky built his fledgling spy group into the powerful and feared Cheka, forerunner to the NKVD and KGB.

Left: Triple portrait of Cardinal Richelieu; right: Mary Queen of Scots; opposite page: Sir Francis Walsingham, spymaster for Queen Elizabeth I of England.

Walsingham's most notorious act was to forge part of a letter from Elizabeth's Catholic cousin, Mary Stuart, Queen of Scots. Walshingham, himself a devotee of codes and ciphers, instructed cryptographer Thomas Phelippes to add a coded postscript to the letter that outlined a plot to assassinate Queen Elizabeth.

As long as Mary Stuart was alive, Walsingham feared she might serve as figurehead for an invasion. As a result of this fabricated evidence, Mary, Queen of Scots, lost her head.

"Knowledge is never too dear."
—Spymaster Sir Francis Walsingham to Queen Elizabeth I

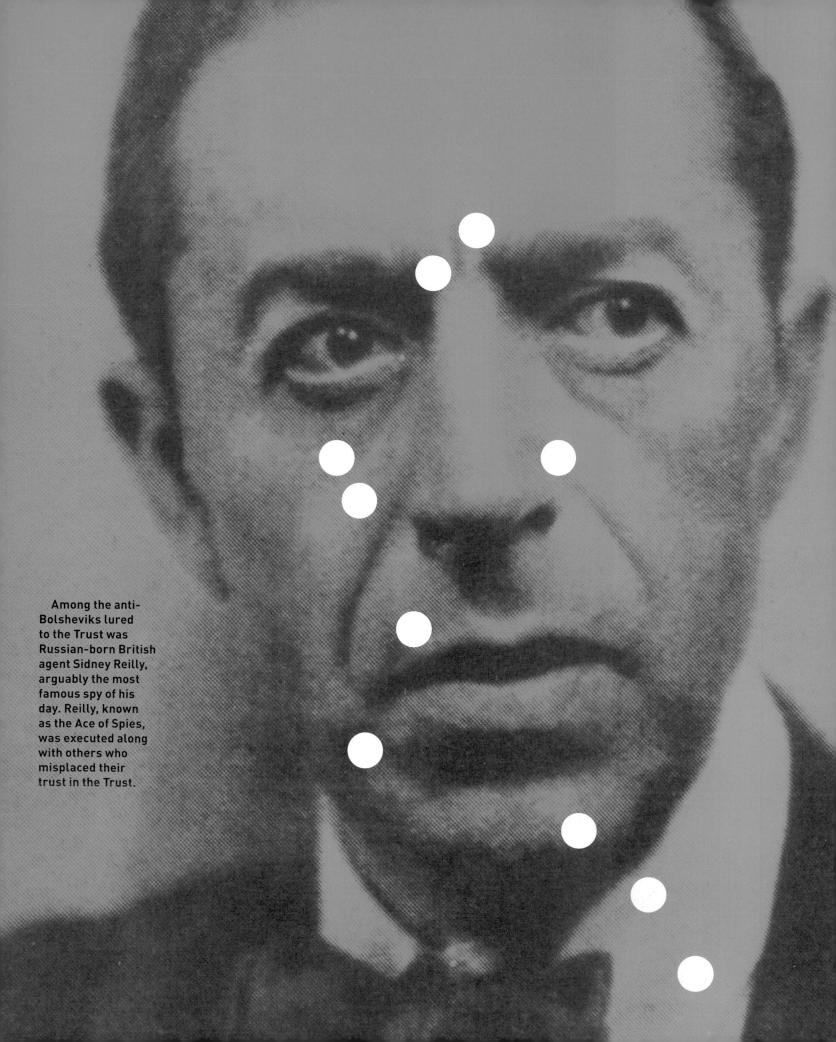

Among the anti-Bolsheviks lured to the Trust was Russian-born British agent Sidney Reilly, arguably the most famous spy of his day. Reilly, known as the Ace of Spies, was executed along with others who misplaced their trust in the Trust.

The main threat to Dzerzhinsky was the great number of Russian émigrés and royalists plotting to overthrow the Bolshevik regime. He solved the problem of infiltrating all the opposition organizations by creating one of his own. The Trust, as it was called, was so successful in carrying out small acts of sabotage against the new government while keeping one step ahead of the Bolshevik retaliation that agents from nearly every other resistance group began collaborating with it.

Not all spymasters are brilliant and cunning, of course. Take Allan Pinkerton of the detective agency Pinkertons. The son of a Scottish policeman, he built an intelligence network for Union general George B. McClellan during the Civil War. Whether it was because his experience had been limited to chasing railroad bandits or because he knew what McClellan wanted to hear, Pinkerton provided wildly exaggerated numbers of Confederate troop levels, which convinced the general to sit on his hands. McClellan was fired by President Lincoln for having, as he put it, a case of the "slows."

Pinkerton committed an unpardonable blunder during the Civil War that cost him three agents. When one of his spies did not appear for a scheduled rendezvous, Pinkerton sent two more to the man's home in Richmond, Virginia. Conspicuous in their dress, the agents were immediately arrested. They betrayed the third agent who, it turned out, had only been sick with the flu.

GEORGE WASHINGTON— America's First Spymaster

Washington's growing sophistication in covert action was displayed in his dealings with a man accused of being a British spy. Rather than arrest him, Washington invited the man to dinner, where he was allowed to steal a document that inflated Washington's troop strength. Those numbers persuaded the British to cancel an attack.

George Washington's journey from gentleman farmer to one of the eighteenth century's most successful spymasters was equal parts desperation and opportunity. His desperation was a result of the near annihilation of his Continental army in his first battle as its commander. The British managed to sneak a sizable force past his Brooklyn defenses (a borough Washington had originally surveyed) to inflict fourteen hundred casualties on his troops. If not for British general William Howe's surprising sluggishness, which let Washington's troops escape (he assumed they'd come to their senses in time), the war might have ended in August 1776.

Four months later, in the cold and snow of Valley Forge, things looked even worse for Washington. His soldiers were deserting at an alarming rate, popular support for the war had plummeted, the Continental Congress had fled Philadelphia for Baltimore, and merchants were refusing to accept the new Continental dollar. In a letter to his brother that December, Washington wrote, "I think the game is pretty near up."

But salvation arrived one frozen afternoon in the form of Irishman John Honeyman, who intentionally ran his cow past Washington's camp sentries, who wrestled him to the ground. The guards, guessing that Honeyman, a known Tory sympathizer, was operating as a British spy, brought him to General Washington. They were only half right. Honeyman was one of the first secret agents George Washington had hired, and the information he now produced validated that choice. The British army had left the nearby city of Trenton guarded only by Hessian troops under the command of a drunkard who had so little respect for America's "country clowns" that he hadn't erected fortifications or dispatched scouts.

After arranging Honeyman's escape, Washington immediately made plans to attack. At dawn on Christmas Day, Washington crossed the Delaware with twenty-four hundred men and caught the Hessians still asleep. He took Trenton without a single American fatality. Emboldened by this success, Washington scored another victory at Princeton a few days later. These two victories, though barely more than skirmishes, boosted morale enough to keep the Revolution alive until spring.

Among agents Washington recruited and trained were James Rivington, the publisher of a rabidly pro-British newspaper in New York City, and a tailor named Hercules Mulligan, who literally charmed the pants off British officers who frequented his Manhattan shop. (Mulligan passed along details of two plots to kidnap the general.)

Washington's greatest intelligence success in the Revolutionary War helped hasten its end. In 1779 America's French allies attacked British forces at Yorktown, Virginia. For the plan to succeed, Washington's troops needed to join the French and close the trap, while keeping the British fleet at bay in New York. To that end, Washington threatened an attack on New York City. Using tactics that would be copied 165 years later during preparations for the Allied D-Day invasion, he established a camp on the New Jersey shore with a huge kitchen and many tents and campfires. He then assembled every boat he could find to make it appear as though an invasion was imminent. False reports and documents, which the British intercepted, further supported the notion. After an all-night march, Washington reached Yorktown before the British could react to the deception. It would be the deciding engagement of the war.

Opposite page: General George Washington's letter to Nathaniel Sackett.

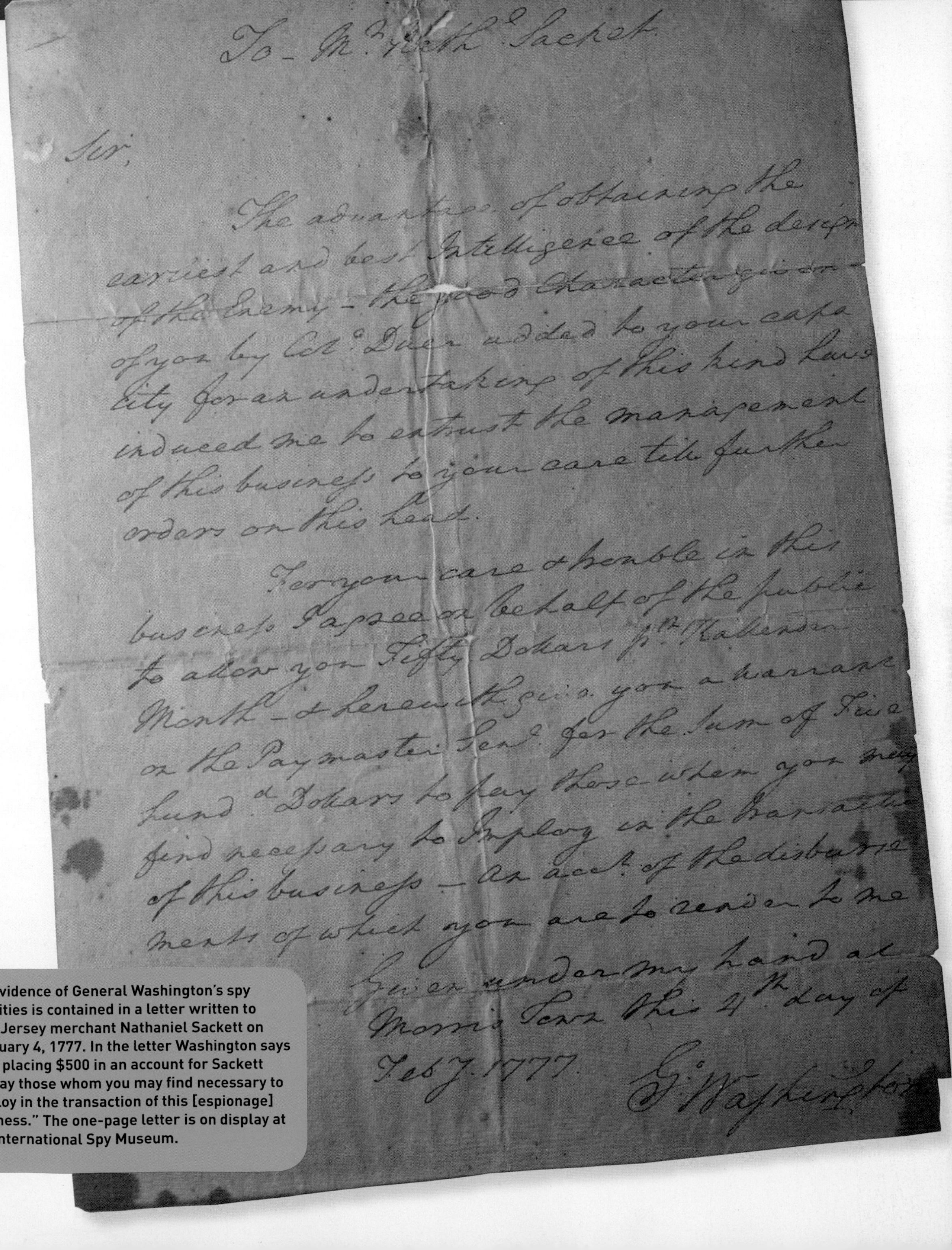

To - M.r Nath.l Sackett.

Sir,

The advantage of obtaining the earliest and best Intelligence of the designs of the Enemy — the good character given of you by Col.o Duer added to your capacity for an undertaking of this kind have induced me to entrust the management of this business to your care till further orders on this head.

For your care & trouble in this business I agree on behalf of the public to allow you Fifty Dollars p.r Kalendar Month — & herewith give you a warrant on the Pay master Gen.l for the Sum of Five hund.d Dollars to pay those whom you may find necessary to imploy in the transaction of this business — An acc.t of the disbursements of which you are to render to me

Given under my hand at Morris Town this 4.th day of Feb.y 1777.

G.o Washington

Evidence of General Washington's spy activities is contained in a letter written to New Jersey merchant Nathaniel Sackett on February 4, 1777. In the letter Washington says he is placing $500 in an account for Sackett "to pay those whom you may find necessary to employ in the transaction of this [espionage] business." The one-page letter is on display at the International Spy Museum.

PAUL BANTE

MAX BLANK

ALFRED E. BROKHOF

RUDOLPH EBELING

RICHARD EICHENLAUB

HEINRICH CARL EILE

JOSEF KLEIN

HARTWIG KLEISS

HEINRICH CLAUSING

CONRADINE DOLD

FREDERICK DUQUE

RECRUITING THE PERFECT SPY

PAUL FEHSE

EDMUND CARL HEINE

FELIX JAHNKE

HERMAN LANG

EVELYN CLAYTON LEWIS

RENE EMANUEL MEZ

So you want to be a spy. Well, who doesn't? The (alleged) glamour and glory, the dashboard rockets on your Aston Martin DB8 sports car, the chance to trade a job tracking office supply inventory for one that might save the world. But do you have the right stuff?

Here's a test. You're carrying secret documents for the Allies in German-occupied France during World War II. But when you get off the train in Avignon, you find yourself facing a line of nasty-looking security officers checking everyone's identity papers. Do you:

    a. Turn and run.
    b. Pull your hat over your eyes (don't worry, nearly everyone
       wore hats back then).
    c. Whip out your ink-pen pistol and start firing.

If you answered yes to any of those, it's back to your day job. Here is how SOE (Special Operations Executive) agent Francis Cammaerts handled that exact situation during the war. Knowing that the Germans were afraid of contracting tuberculosis, Cammaerts bit his lip until it bled, made a hacking cough, and spit blood at the feet of the officers. They parted like the Red Sea to let him pass.

In truth there is no perfect spy candidate, at least not one for all occasions. During a war you might want a pistol-and-parachute type, while at other times someone with Middle East language skills or a degree in chemical engineering would top the list.

There are a few basic requirements—the ability to follow orders, an eye for detail, and intuitiveness—though even these rudiments are sometimes ignored for the sake of expediency. During World War II, for example, the Allies recruited a group of agents who had never shown any regard for obeying orders. Mafia members from New York and Chicago, who hated Mussolini for outlawing their organization in Italy, were used to prepare the way for a landing in Sicily.

At first blush it might appear that the best espionage recruit would be a volunteer, one who asks nothing more than to perform a patriot's duty. Another alternative for a recruit might be a highly-placed defector who

"He was one of the cleverest creatures I ever saw. His style of patriotic lying was sublime, it amounted to genius."—*Charles A. Dana, Assistant Secretary of War during the Civil War writing about Union spy Richard Montgomery*

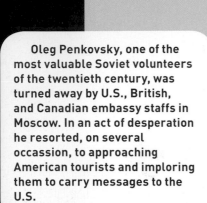

crosses over with sacks of state secrets from his homeland. But both volunteers and defectors make spymasters nervous. There is always the chance that such a willing volunteer may have an ulterior motive. For example, the eager volunteer may actually be trying to pass off disinformation or he may be part of a larger deception. For this reason genuine defectors are sometimes turned away by wary intelligence agencies.

Another reason the walk-in arouses suspicion is the very nature of espionage work. Active field agents must develop a split personality— the ability to be cunning and withholding with adversaries, yet loving with family and friends. With the greatly exaggerated perception of spies as irresistible lovers and licensed killers, the profession can attract what intelligence psychologists have labeled the "psychopathic spy personality," a type that tends to leave a bloody mess.

It is often the case that spymasters are more comfortable with an agent they've targeted, worked, and recruited. Sometimes all it takes is an appeal to patriotism, but just as often money closes the deal. However, an offer of money for intelligence can create a market for false information. During the Revolutionary War the British army in Quebec, fearing an attack, offered money for related intelligence. Many people volunteered information, and so much of it was false that the British purchased only confusion. The misleading prewar intelligence from several sources about Iraqi weapons of mass destruction may fall into that category.

There is another type of recruitment known as a false flag. An agent will represent himself as working for a country that might have some appeal for the target. Israelis, for example, have been known to recruit Arab agents by pretending to represent the CIA.

As valuable as defectors may be, intelligence agencies much prefer "penetration" agents, those willing to remain in place and provide a continuing stream of current information. KGB general Oleg Kalugin, who recruited and managed a galaxy of spies during his thirty-two years in the KGB, supervised one particularly valuable spy ring headed by U.S. Navy Warrant Officer John A. Walker. With help from his son and brother, Walker provided the USSR with codes to decrypt all messages sent from U.S. Navy headquarters in Washington, DC, to its ships and nuclear submarines around the world. Kalugin says it was much easier to recruit western spies in the 1930s to work for the Soviet Union for ideological reasons.

"The Soviet system in its original form was full of lofty ideals," says Kalugin, who is now an American citizen and lives in a suburb of Washington, DC, where he writes and does consulting. "It was a paradise on earth based on social justice, the nobility of people, the brotherhood of nations. The idea was great but the implementation was lousy."

After Soviet tanks rolled into Czechoslovakia in 1968 to halt a reform movement, Kalugin says the last of that goodwill for the Soviet system finally disappeared. He began targeting Soviets living in the United States who might be having financial trouble and more radical leftwing groups. "We now had problems finding ideological substitutes. But we found substitutes, people who understood that the next world war would bring total annihilation, and national liberation movement in third world countries."

And yes, he admits, there were occasions when other "pressures" might be applied. As he once told an audience in Las Vegas, "Catching people with their pants down was a prime way of compromising and recruiting them."

The way that this worked was to target someone in a valuable position who had a weakness for alcohol, sex, drugs, or gambling. The person would be supplied with his or her chosen vice while hidden cameras clicked away.

One of the more innovative twentieth-century spymasters was blackmailed into betraying his own country, a betrayal that helped spark the beginning of World War I. Colonel Alfred Redl, the head of Austrian counterintelligence and a secret homosexual, was provided with young men and money by Russian agents, who then sprang the honey trap. Among the intelligence documents Redl gave Russia was a detailed Austrian plan for invading Serbia in the event of hostilities.

In the 1980s U.S. Marine Corps sergeant Clayton Lonetree was blackmailed by the Soviet Union into handing over classified documents to a KGB agent. The leverage applied was photographs of Lonetree in a sexual relationship with a female Soviet agent. This type of snare—using sex as a tool of blackmail—is known as a honey trap.

Colonel Alfred Redl.

PAUL BANTE

MAX BLANK

ALFRED E. BROKHOFF

HEINRICH CLAUSING

CONRADINE DOLD

FREDERICK DUQUESNE

RUDOLPH EBELING

RICHARD EICHENLAUB

HEINRICH CARL EILERS

PAUL FEHSE

EDMUND CARL HEINE

FELIX JAHNKE

GUSTAVE KAERCHER

JOSEF KLEIN

HARTWIG KLEISS

HERMAN LANG

EVELYN CLAYTON LEWIS

RENE EMANUEL MEZENEN

CARL REUPER

EVERETT ROEDER

PAUL SCHOLZ

GEORGE GOTTLOB SCHUH

ERWIN WILHELM SIEGLER

OSCAR STABLER

HEINRICH STADE

LILLY STEIN

FRANZ JOSEPH STIGLER

ERICK STRUNK

LEO WAALEN

ADOLF WALISCHEWSKI

ELSE WEUSTENFELD

AXEL WHEELER-HILL

BERTRAM W. ZENZINGER

THE
33 CONVICTED MEMBERS
OF THE
DUQUESNE
SPY RING

In 1914, when a mentally unstable Serbian student shot Archduke Franz Ferdinand, Austria did invade that country. But because of Serbia's familiarity with Austria's order of battle, its smaller army was able to beat back the Austrians. Instead of a quick end, the stalemate gave allies of both sides time to offer support, resulting in the Great War.

Redl was found out after Austrian agents he'd trained intercepted a large amount of money in envelopes addressed to his post office box. He was given a pistol, which he used to commit suicide after writing a note:

Levity and passion have destroyed me. Pray for me. I pay with my life for my sins.

Below: German American William Sebold with Frederick Duquesne. Sebold served as double-agent for the FBI and helped close down Germany's spy network in America.

Opposite page: Convicted members of the Duquesne spy ring.

Blackmail sometimes backfires, as was the case with one loyal German American, William Sebold. After entering the United States illegally in 1922, Sebold had become a successful aircraft mechanic and worked on some of America's most powerful new planes. During a visit to Germany in 1939, Sebold was approached by Gestapo agents who threatened to inform the United States of his immigration status unless he provided information about America's aviation industry. After two months of training, Sebold was sent back to the United States, where he immediately contacted the FBI and convinced officers of his willingness to play the double agent.

Sebold became an invaluable link in the Duquesne spying operation, which numbered dozens of German agents. As the operator of a clandestine radio transmitter, Sebold handled a high volume of sensitive material, which he copied for his American handlers. With his help, the FBI closed down Germany's spy network in America and arrested thirty agents.

4.

BUILDING THE PERFECT SPY

With the ideal candidate recruited, the next step to creating a serviceable spy is basic training. What type of training will depend upon the job required. An agent spying for India's sixteenth-century Mogul ruler Akbar, for example, needed little more than a good memory and strong legs. Each day Akbar sent his four thousand agents into his kingdom to look and listen for evidence of dissension or revolt.

Contrast this with the skill set required of Jedburgh agents during World War II. Jedburgh is a Scottish city where the OSS trained teams of agents to parachute into France. These Allied operatives, referred to as "Jeds," supported by American and British intelligence, were dropped behind enemy lines in Europe to make contact with local agents, encrypt gathered intelligence and transmit it by wireless, blow up rail yards and bridges, and engage enemy troops in hand-to-hand combat. Such missions required training in every aspect of combat and espionage.

Intelligence services in nearly every country have some form of spy training, often tailored to the needs of the time. In the early twentieth century Germany had a five-month program that emphasized trigonometry, topography, and drawing—training suited for sketching enemy deployments and fortifications.

By World War II agents needed instruction in the use of weapons, Morse code, radio repair, cipher systems, and the making of microdots (miniaturized photographs) from headache powder, vodka, and the cellophane from cigarette packs.

"In war time, truth is so precious that she should always be attended by a bodyguard of lies."—*British Prime Minister, Winston Churchill*

Top: Tweezers and a microdot; opposite page: Spies use a special light to illuminate once-invisible fingerprints.

One of the more interesting U.S. spy schools in the 1940s was located in Maryland farm country (at Congressional Country Club) twenty miles north of Washington, DC. Agents were taught code breaking, lock picking, and silent killing, as well as the use of radio transmitters, techniques for establishing covers, recruiting agents, and falsifying documents. As a graduation test the prospective agent was required to penetrate a defense plant and steal information. (The FBI and local police were alerted ahead of time to prevent unplanned shootouts and newspaper headlines.)

A long-secret but now celebrated commando training facility called Camp-X was located in Canada on the shores of Lake Ontario about thirty miles from the U.S. border. Opened in 1941, the camp trained Americans, British, Canadians, Yugoslavians, Italians, Romanians, and Hungarians in

British author Ian Fleming, a graduate of Camp-X.

the skills needed to operate behind enemy lines. Among the graduates of the camp were William Colby, who later headed the CIA, and Ian Fleming—author of the James Bond novels, but then a British naval intelligence officer. In a biography of Fleming, writer John Pearson recounts Fleming being given an assignment to go into a Camp-X building and shoot a man he'd find hiding in an upstairs bedroom as a test of his nerve. Fleming stood outside the door for a while, then left. He later said, "You know, I couldn't really kill a man that way." But his fictional characters certainly could.

It's interesting to note that some of the tradecraft techniques taught sixty years ago are still relevant today—how to maintain surveillance, set up dead drops to provide documents or payment, and take the most basic precautions, such as always keeping a car clean of fingerprints.

At a facility officially known as "Armed Forces Experimental Training Activity," and unofficially known as the CIA's Camp Peary (aka the Farm) near Williamsburg, Virginia, case officer recruits known as Career Trainees undertake an eighteen-week course in Flaps and Seals (opening and then resealing letters), Picks and Locks, Disguises, and Photography. They are also taught the art of collecting information at cocktail parties as well as the correct way to write reports, arrange meetings with assets, and determine if they're being followed.

More robust paramilitary training is also provided by the CIA. A program jokingly called "Outward Bound with guns" puts trainees in woods and swampland, where they must evade hunters. Some recruits are also held in jail without food or water and interrogated for an extended time.

Contemporary agents still use passwords, wear distinctive lapel pins, or carry prearranged objects such as a glove or cane to identify themselves. Signals used to indicate when a dead drop has been filled have not changed significantly over time. When John Walker was arrested in 1985 at a hotel after leaving a dead drop in Maryland, he'd placed a soda can beside a utility pole to indicate there was material to be picked up. The documents were inside a trash bag at another utility pole.

Former CIA officer Edward Lee Howard, who defected to the Soviet Union in 1985 while under suspicion that he was passing secrets to the USSR, credited a technique he learned in training school for helping him escape. With his home under FBI surveillance, Howard went to dinner with his wife, Mary (who also worked for the CIA). On their way home, with Mary driving, he used a broom handle, wig, and baseball cap to make a dummy for the front seat, then jumped from the car. Once inside the garage, his wife called a number that had an answering machine and played a tape of her husband arranging a meeting for the following morning. The FBI, eavesdropping on that phone call, was confident of Howard's whereabouts, which gave him a twenty-four-hour head start.

TOOLS OF THE TRADE

Some of the more interesting gadgets and tools used by spies to collect, conceal, or deliver information include the following:

A wristwatch camera.

These KGB hollow coins easily concealed microfilm and microdots. They were opened by inserting a needle into a tiny hole in the front of the coin.

OSS suitcase radio.

The device, shaped to resemble a large piece of coal, was hollowed out to conceal explosives. Using the camouflage kit, an agent painted the shell to match the color of the local coal. When the coal was shoveled into a boiler, the device detonated.

This hollow battery could be used to conceal film or even small cameras.

A hollow shaving cream can, with just enough cream to fool an inspector.

A film container in a can of talcum powder has an internal electrical circuit that fires a flashbulb to ruin the film if opened improperly.

YARDLEY
Invisible Tale
FOR
AFTER SHAVING

This dog doo transmitter effectively camouflaged a homing beacon.

A dead drop spike was used to hold film or documents, then driven into the ground and marked with string.

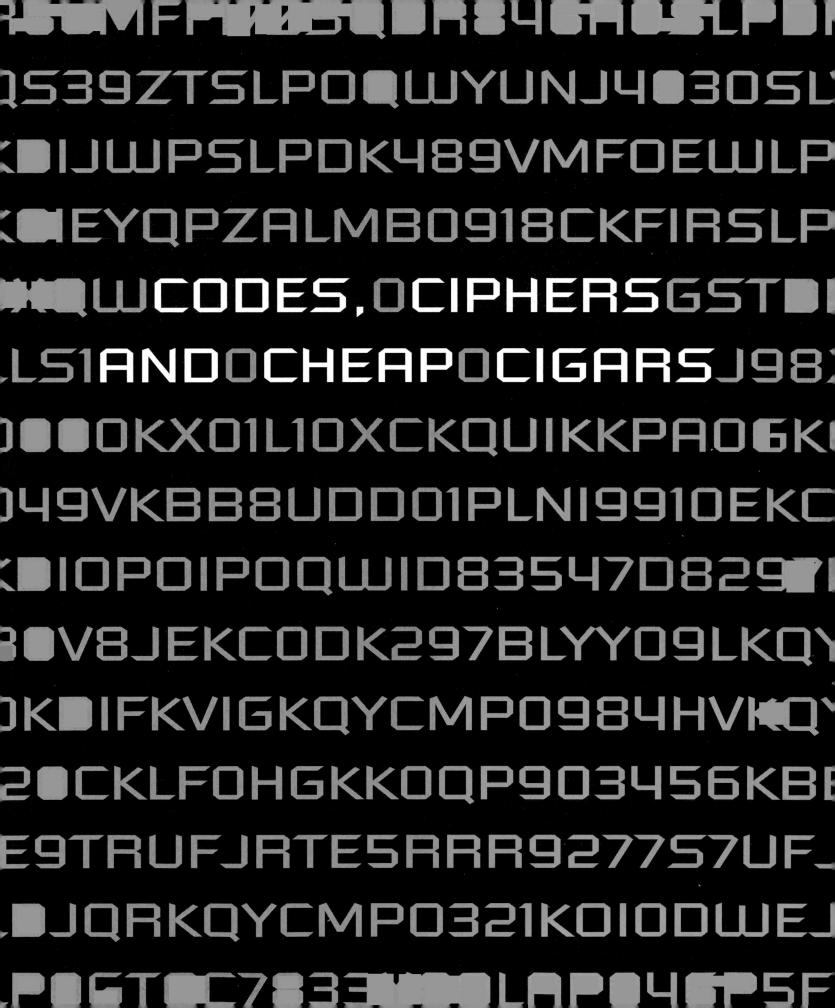

When the eleventh-century Chinese spymasters had a secret message to deliver, they sometimes wrote it on a piece of silk, coated it with wax, and swallowed it—a foolproof method of concealment as long as delivery was within a day's walk. Giovanni Porta, a sixteenth-century Italian scientist, concealed his messages inside hard-boiled eggs by writing them on the outer shell with a mixture of vinegar and alum (one pint to one ounce). The ink seeped through the shell onto the white of the egg, where it could be read only after removing the shell.

For messages that didn't need to get anywhere fast, the Greek historian Herodotus described a method of shaving an agent's head and writing on his scalp. The message could only be delivered after his hair had grown long enough to conceal it.

The problem with hiding messages is that when one is found, so too is its content. This is why kings and queens, generals, and cheating spouses encouraged the evolution of cryptography, a method of hiding not only the message but also its meaning by using substitution codes, ciphers, and letter scrambling.

One of the simplest cryptography methods was invented by the sixteenth-century mathematician Girolamo Cardano. Picture the Cardano Grill as an eight-by-ten-inch piece of cardboard with word-sized pieces cut from it. The writer simply lays the grill over a sheet of paper and writes the message in the empty spaces. Remove the grill and fill the rest of the page with innocuous writing. When the recipient of the message opens the letter, he or she sees the hidden message by putting the same grill over the page.

Alexander the Great wrote messages on a skytale, strips of paper wrapped around a staff of a certain circumference. He then unwound the strips and sent them to his recipients. The writing would have no apparent meaning until the paper was again wrapped around a staff of the same circumference.

Transposition

An anagram that presents words or sentences in scrambled form is a transposition. Another simple variety might use every other letter in a line of letters.

The message DANGER would appear as:
V D N A T N O G P E L R

32

"Knowledge is power."—*Sir Francis Bacon, seventeenth-century poet, scientist, code writer, and spy*

A slightly more sophisticated method, known as a rail fence, uses two parallel lines of letters, switching from one line to the other at intervals known only by the message writer and recipient. Here is how a message would appear, alternating letters from the top to middle rail of the fence at an interval of one:

Enemy approaches

e p e c y t p l r v a o h l s
y n k m s a e p b o x c i e

Codes

The next jump in sophistication involved the use of codes, which simply means substituting one or more words for others. Writing to tell someone that you've recently been pestered by an annoying dog takes on a whole new meaning if *dog* is the code word for "spy" or "saboteur." As long as the writer and recipient have the same codebook and a modicum of sense, codes are a more secure method of sending secret information.

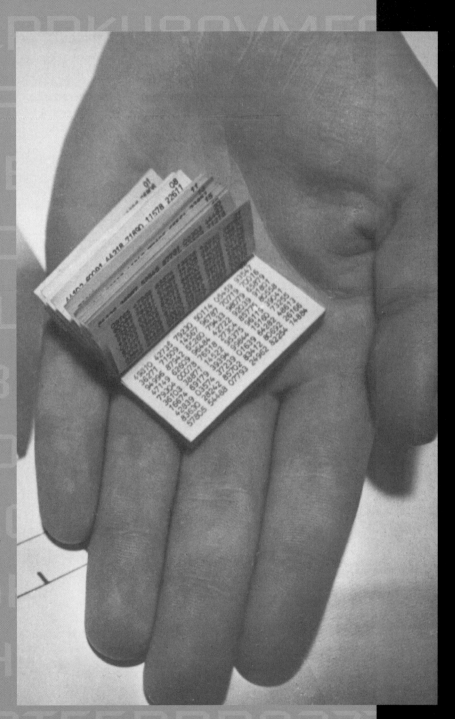

Mini code book from c. 1968.

Navajo Code Talkers

One of the more effective uses of code occurred during World War II when members of the Navajo tribe were recruited by U.S. Marine Corps to send and receive radio messages on battlefields. The Navajo Code Talkers were particularly successful because their language was not written and was virtually impenetrable to anyone outside the tribe. To overcome a problem with the language's lack of military vocabulary, the Navajo created new words to compensate:

Platoon: Mudclan
Fortifications: Cavedwellings
Mortars: Guns that squat
Bombs: Eggs

Navajo Code Talkers operating a radio in dense jungle during World War II.

Ciphers

A cipher is a letter, number, or symbol used as a substitute for other letters or words and is potentially the most sophisticated substitution method for the cryptologist. It is also the most challenging for the person trying to uncover the real meaning of an encrypted message, the cryptanalyst.

Julius Caesar created his own cipher (known not surprisingly as the Caesar Cipher) that substituted one letter of the alphabet for another letter of the same alphabet but shifted forward anywhere from one to twenty-five places. In Caesar Cipher 3, for example, the letter *A* would be represented as the letter *D*, which is three letters forward of *A*. The recipient of the message, naturally, would need to know the key (the number of shifts forward) to translate the message.

Using Caesar Cipher 1 to encrypt this message, each letter in the original message would be represented by the letter that comes after it in the alphabet.

    Send more spears
    Tfoe npsf tqfbst

Substitution Cipher

The next evolution in cipher cryptology came by substituting letters of the alphabet with a random arrangement of letters, numbers, or symbols from the same alphabet. Instead of having only twenty-five possible shifts to consider, the new substitution cipher presented cryptanalysts with an impossibly large number (400,000,000,000,000,000,000,000,000,000) of choices.

Something as simple as the phrase COME HERE would be nearly impossible to decipher without knowing the correct cipher alphabet.

    Plain Alphabet: A B C D E F G H I J K L M N O P Q R S
    Cipher Alphabet: F Z L O Q T R A B I P E N H C D G J K

    Plain Text: C O M E   H E R E
    Cipher Text: L C N Q   A Q J Q

Frequency Analysis

Cryptographers were invincible for two centuries until Arab cryptanalysts studying the Koran once again leveled the playing field. They determined that certain letters in an alphabet are used more often than others (in the English language the dominant letter is *E*), and in a predictable ratio. By charting the relative percentages of each substitution letter's or cipher's appearance in an encrypted page of text, they could reasonably assume which ciphers represented which letters of plain text.

The twentieth-century refinement of the radio brought about the next great advance in cryptology. When messages could be sent instantaneously through the air and intercepted just as easily, cryptologists needed to develop more secure defenses. That meant turning to machines.

The earliest known cryptographic machine is a fifteenth-century cipher disk invented by Italian painter Leon Alberti to code messages for his pope. Two copper disks with alphabets etched on each of their edges were put together, the smaller disk on top. Using the Caesar Cipher shift, one of the disks is rotated from one to twenty-five shifts to the other's alphabet. This disk was still being used during America's Civil War four hundred years later.

Some of the more intense efforts of the Second World War were fought in windowless rooms by men and women trying to decrypt enemy communications. German and Japanese encryption codes and ciphers, produced by incredibly complex machines, were considered invulnerable until Allied cryptographers built fantastic machines of their own to decrypt them.

Confederate Civil War cipher disk.

A seventeenth-century French prisoner who provoked speculation as to his identity for two hundred years was finally unmasked through the breaking of a secret substitution cipher. In books, poetry, and drama the prisoner, who was never seen without a tight-fitting mask, was represented as a member of the royal family, perhaps the twin of French king Louis XIV, who'd been imprisoned to avoid any disputes over rightful ascension to the throne. Everyone from Benjamin Franklin to Alexandre Dumas had a theory. The mystery was apparently solved in 1893 with the cracking of the two-hundred-year-old Great Cipher, whose secrets had been lost during the time of King Louis and had withstood generations of cryptanalysts' efforts. The Man in the Iron Mask, according to a decrypted letter from the king's minister of war, was in fact a military commander who'd shown great cowardice in battle and who in fact wore a velvet mask. But as Simon Singh's *The Code Book* notes, those who believe in conspiracies argued that the encrypted letter was meant to be deciphered to hide the real trail.

Purple cipher machine.

Purple

At a girls' school in Arlington, Virginia, commandeered by the U.S. Army's Signal Intelligence Service during World War II, America's top code breakers William F. Friedman and Frank B. Rowlett led a team that in eighteen months cracked Japan's highest-level diplomatic cipher system. Friedman called his team "Magicians," and so the decrypted communications were known as "Magic." The effort centered on building a machine to mimic the one used by the Japanese, a machine they'd never seen. The first Purple machine (*Purple* was also the name given to the Japanese cipher) was built in 1940, and the first Japane se message successfully translated the following year. In a story that may be apocryphal, Frank Rowlett is said to have celebrated that achievement with a Coca-Cola and the words, "Let's get back to work."

Two years after Purple, British cryptologists and engineers working to decrypt a German machine, known as Lorenz, built Colossus, the world's first programmable, digital electronic computer. After the war it was said that Winston Churchill, apparently afraid of the computer's power, ordered Colossus to be broken into pieces "no bigger than a man's hand."

SPY SHOPS

The first full-time civilian intelligence agency in the United States was not created until 1947, and its birth was hardly trouble-free. President Harry Truman, who had a well-known distrust of secret organizations, disbanded the Office of Strategic Services intelligence unit immediately after World War II and refused all entreaties to form a peacetime agency to collect and evaluate intelligence.

Truman had a lot of support for his position. The armed services, State Department, and FBI, each with its own intelligence service, did not want to relinquish turf to a new and possibly more powerful rival. In arguments that echo contemporary U.S. debates, the FBI's J. Edgar Hoover complained that a new agency would only duplicate his domestic intelligence gathering.

But external events, in particular the expansionist policies of the Soviet Union, created a sense of emergency that existing intelligence services did nothing to allay. The raw, unfiltered, and confusing intelligence provided to Truman persuaded him to change his mind. A naval aide to Truman later recalled the president's explanation for creating the Central Intelligence Agency: "I had information coming at me from 200 different sources," said Truman. "I wanted someone to boil it down for me."

President Truman's intrinsic distrust of intelligence services represented an attitude as old as the nation. Many Americans considered spying to be sneaky and underhanded, like hitting below the belt. That attitude was exemplified by President Woodrow Wilson, who threatened to fire his entire general staff before the start of World War I after learning they'd been making contingency plans for an attack on Germany.

Other nations shared some of that same distrust of secret organizations. Great Britain, for example, did not establish its own full-time intelligence service until 1909 and only then because a fiction writer by the name of William Le Queux wrote a novel, *Spies of the Kaiser*, as well as a series of alarmist newspaper articles that whipped up a fear that German spies were hiding behind every British hedgerow. Although the British prime minister called Le Queux a "pernicious scaremonger," public pressure led to the creation of Her Majesty's Secret Service Bureau.

Herbert O. Yardley, the pioneer of American code breaking, lost all of the State Department's funding for his American Cipher Bureau in 1929 after he provided the new secretary of state, Henry Stimson, with decoded Japanese documents. Stimson sniffed, "Gentlemen do not read each other's mail." Yardley got his revenge two years later with the publication of a tell-all best seller, *The American Black Chamber*.

CIA shield.

Le Queux claimed to have a list of German infiltrators (allegedly "the Hidden Hand"), which included members of Parliament, writers, and members of half a dozen government agencies including the Foreign and War Offices. But like U.S. senator Joseph McCarthy half a century later, he never disclosed those names.

"It is bad Christianity, bad sportsmanship, bad sense to challenge the integrity of the Soviet government
—Joseph E. Davies, U.S. ambassador to USSR in 1937

Acronyms of International Intelligence Agencies

Badge worn by KGB agent.

- **ABWEHR:** German military intelligence, 1921–1944.

- **BCRA:** Free French intelligence service during World War II, established by Charles de Gaulle, 1940–1945.

- **BND (Bundesnachichtendiest):** West German intelligence, established in 1956.

- **CHEKA (Chrezvychanaya Kommissya po Borbe S Kontr-revolutsyey):** Soviet secret state police and intelligence organization, 1917–1922.

- **CIA:** U.S. Central Intelligence Agency, established in 1947.

- **DGSE (Direction Générale de la Sécurité Extérieure):** French intelligence.

- **DS (Daijavna Sugurnost):** Bulgarian secret service established in 1949.

- **FBI (Feberal Bureau of Investigation),** U.S. domestic counterintelligence service, established in 1935.

- **FSB (Federal'naya Sluzhba Bezopasnosti)** Russian federal security, established in 1993.

- **GPU (Gosudarstvennaye Politsheskoye Upravlenye):** Soviet secret police and intelligence service, 1922–1923.

- **GRU (Glavnaye Razvedyvatelnoye Upravlenye):** Soviet Union military intelligence, established in 1920.

- **KGB (Komitat Gosudarstvennoy Bezopastnosti):** Soviet secret police and intelligence organization, 1954–1991.

- **KISS:** South Korean Intelligence and Security Service, established in 1953.

- **MAD (Militärischer Abschirm-Dienst):** Military counterintelligence for the Bundeswehr, Federal German Armed Forces, established in 1984.

- **MI5:** British counterintelligence, established in 1909.

- **MI6:** British intelligence, established in 1911.

- **MOSSAD (ha-Mossad le-Modiin ule-Tafkidim Meyuhadim):** Israel's Institute for Intelligence and Special Tasks, established in 1951.

- **NAICHO (Naikaku Chosashitsu Betsushitsu):** Japanese national intelligence service.

- **NKVD (Narodniy Kommissariat Vnyutrennikh Dyel):** Soviet secret police and intelligence organization, 1934–1946.

- **NSA:** U.S. National Security Agency, signals intelligence organization, established in 1952.

- **OGPU (Oby'edinyonnoye Gals u darstvenn O y Politicheskoye):** Soviet secret police and intelligence organization, 1923–1934.

- **OSS:** U.S. Office of Strategic Services, American intelligence during World War II, 1940–1946.

- **SAVAK (Sazamane Etelaat va Amniate Kechvar):** Iranian Security and Intelligence Service, 1957–1979.

- **SOE (Special Operations Executive)** British WWII organization to foster resistance in German occcupied lands, 1940–1946.

STASI cap.

- **SVR (Suzhba Vneshney Razvedki)** Russian foreign intelligence, established in 1992.

- **STASI (Mfinisterium für Staatssicherheit):** East German security and intelligence service during the Cold War, 1950–1989.

France's most public intelligence blunder came in 1985, when government agents sank the Greenpeace environmental ship *Rainbow Warrior*, killing a photographer on board. The ship was part of a flotilla designed to block France from testing nuclear weapons on New Caledonia. French agents, who fixed underwater mines to the *Rainbow*'s hull while it was anchored in Auckland, New Zealand, left an obvious trail leading to the French embassy.

Before the Berlin Wall came down, East Germany's notorious STASI police employed ninety thousand agents and controlled 173,000 registered informers, roughly one for every hundred citizens. Vera Wollenberger, who'd lost her teaching job and been imprisoned because of STASI harassment, was elected to East Germany's Parliament in 1990, one year after the wall was dismantled. She helped pass a law giving citizens the right to look at their STASI files. In her own file she discovered that the person who'd been informing on her to the STASI was her husband, soon to be her ex-husband.

Modern professional civilian intelligence services were soon established in Germany, Russia and eventually nearly every other nation in what became one of the twentieth century's great growth industries. That growth was likely inevitable given the advent of truly global wars, and it was made more practical by the advances in communication.

Every nation's intelligence service is shaped by that country's strategic interests and specific history. France's DGSE, with roots reaching back to the French Revolution and even further back to Cardinal Richelieu, was considered one of the world's best intelligence agencies at the start of World War I.

But France's occupation by the Nazis, and the collaboration of Frenchmen in the Vichy government, led to deep divisions in that country regarding national institutions, particularly intelligence agencies. This polarity was not helped by subsequent intelligence failures in Vietnam and Algeria.

The German intelligence community has long been an amalgam of as many disperate parts as a good jigsaw puzzle. The modern country, which has changed shape several times over the centuries, has often been at war with itself. During World War II, for example, some of the highest-ranking intelligence officers of the ABWEHR provided intelligence to British agents while simultaneously plotting to assassinate Hitler. During the 1950s, after Germany had been divided in two, East German intelligence depended to a large extent on the Soviet Union, while the CIA helped establish a West German secret service, the BND. German reunification in 1990 provided the BND with an intelligence bonanza that led to the uncovering of scores of Communist moles and double agents.

For roughly fifteen years after the 1917 Revolution, Russia focused its intelligence efforts internally, spying on its own citizens, imprisoning or executing millions. Decades later, citizens brought in for questioning were lucky if they ever emerged from the interogator's office. Hidden behind the wooden front of his office cabinet doors were stairs that led deep into the heart of Butyrka Prison, the most feared symbol of Stalin's communist purges.

When Soviet intelligence was turned outward, it proved to be nearly as brutally efficient. Some say Russians learned the art of spying from Genghis Khan, the master of a ruthless and far-flung spy network during his occupation of Russia. The Soviet intelligence services were particularly adept at recruiting and managing penetration agents and for their patience in waiting, sometimes years, for those agents to rise to a position with access to valuable intelligence.

But in Russia's history of occupation by foreign armies lay the seed of its greatest intelligence weakness—a distrust that sometimes sabotaged

УДОСТОВѢРЕНІЕ.

Предъявитель сего, изображенный на фотографической карточкѣ *Комендантъ*

Губревилгома тов

Пален,

Коему разрѣшается проживать во всѣхъ пунктахъ Могил. губ. названному лицу всѣ начальствующія лица, всѣ воинскіе чины, Совѣты рабочихъ и Крестьянскихъ депутатовъ и общественныя организаціи обязаны въ случаѣ обращеніи къ нимъ оказывать содѣйствіе во всемъ при исполненіи имъ возложенныхъ на него служебныхъ обязанностей, что подписью и приложеніемъ *печати удостовѣ-*

Предсѣдатель

Мог. Губ. Чрезвыч. ком. по борьбѣ съ контр-революц., спекул. и саботажемъ

Секретарь

№ *16*

мая 16 дня 1918 г.

Cheka Secret Police credentials.

the best efforts of its own spy networks. Successful Soviet spymasters and agents working in the West were routinely brought home, and sometimes jailed, on the suspicion that living too long in the West had tainted them.

During Joseph Stalin's reign, agents reporting unwelcomed intelligence were ignored or charged with treason.

Japan, home to ninja and samurai warriors able to make themselves almost invisible, did not formally establish an intelligence service until 1878. But within two decades that intelligence service was sophisticated enough to play the decisive role in successful wars against China and Russia.

The Russo-Japanese War, when the Japanese pushed Russia out of Manchuria, involved Japan's hiring both Chinese workers who worked for Russians to provide information, and Manchurian natives to apply muscle. By the time Japan invaded, its military leaders knew the placement of every Russian troop and armament. When Russia belatedly sent a war fleet of thirty-eight ships to retake the peninsula, Japan was waiting with torpedo boats that sank thirty-four of them.

BARBAROSSA was the German code name for its invasion of the Soviet Union in 1941. The encrypted plans for that invasion were intercepted and deciphered by British, American, Yugoslav, and Swedish intelligence sources and passed to Stalin. One of the Soviet Union's embedded spies in Britain's intelligence services corroborated those reports. British prime minister Winston Churchill sent a personal message to Stalin warning of the attack. Finally the USSR's own military intelligence verified the same information. But Stalin refused to believe any of it, leaving his Red Army at a great disadvantage when Germany did invade.

Medals and documents awarded to NKVD agents for exemplary service.

One of Japan's best agents in Manchuria was a Spanish watch salesman who sent coded messages via a Chinese agent, who hid them inside his hollow gold teeth.

The same detailed intelligence was used by the expansionist Japanese government during World War II. In 1932, nine years before the surprise attack on Pearl Harbor, Japanese agents were already in Hawaii gathering information on shipping and naval strength. The Japanese were farsighted enough to send men to Hawaii, ostensibly to work as loggers, but actually to cut crude landing strips in the woods near Pearl Harbor.

One flaw in Japanese intelligence before World War II was the belief that hostilities would end quickly. When they did not, Japan's intelligence service, which had little code-breaking expertise, was forced to make decisions based on best guesses rather than hard facts.

At the end of World War II, as agents for Soviet Communism and Western democracy raced to divide the world into competing camps, intelligence agencies became more proactive and cold blooded. Russian and American intelligence services in particular squared off in Eastern Europe, Africa, Central America, and South America, arming indigenous populations and spending great sums of money to throw elections and otherwise influence events abroad.

As the Cold War heated up, some tactics, employed by the CIA and FBI, which included assassination attempts, domestic spying, interference in the political affairs of foreign countries, and even mind control, concerned the public in the United States. As a result of congressional hearings chaired by Senator Frank Church and Congressman Otis Pike, the U.S. attorney general was required to concur on some major covert actions.

After the breakup of the Soviet Union in 1991, economic espionage made headlines as nations vied for market share in the increasingly global economy by snooping on former enemies and current friends. Nations no longer expelled one another's embassy personnel for stealing state secrets, but rather for taking industrial ones.

As serious as economic espionage may be—and the American Society for Industrial Security estimates that U.S. industry loses as much as $60 billion a year as a result of it—the role of domestic and foreign intelligence agencies, so recently engaged in a war for the world's very survival, seemed somehow diminished to be occupied with the theft of computer chips.

The events of September 11, 2001, and the subsequent war on terrorism, redirected the mission of international spy agencies. But as former director of the CIA James Woolsey has stated, the new reality demands new strategies:

> *We've slain a large dragon but we now live in a jungle filled with a bewildering variety of poisonous snakes, and in many ways the dragon was easier to keep track of.*

© LUIS JIMENEZ '02

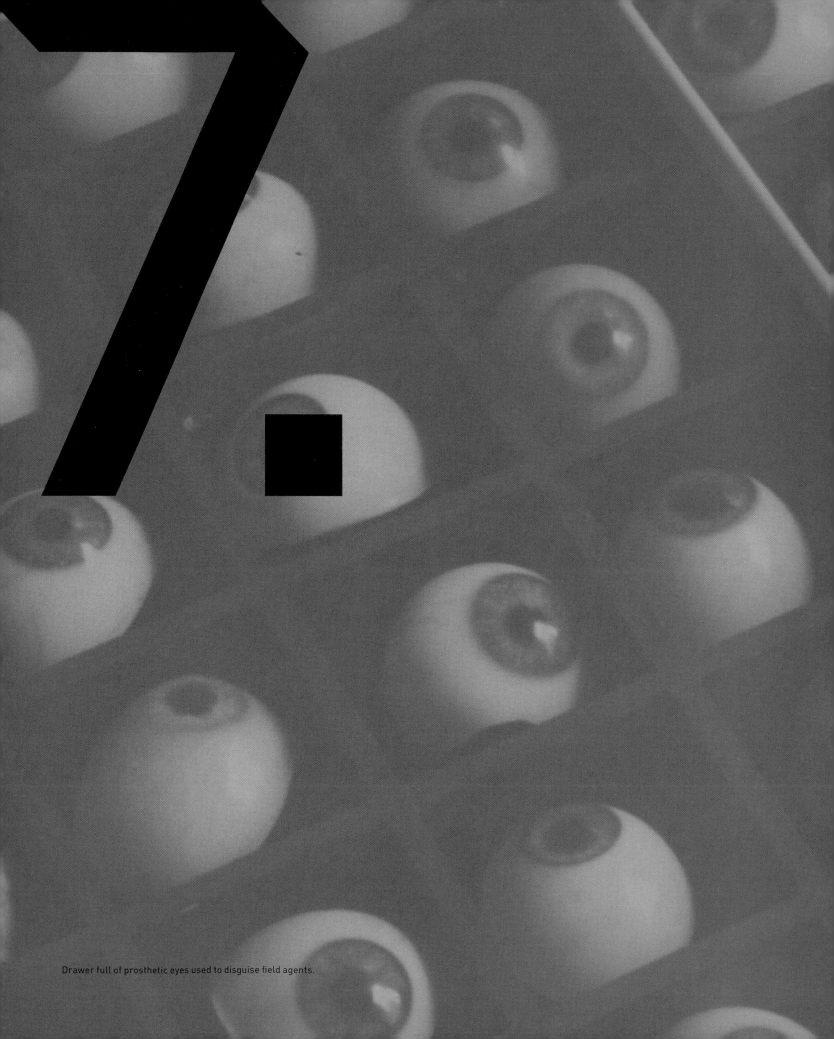

Drawer full of prosthetic eyes used to disguise field agents.

COVERS AND DISGUISES

Pocket litter: Items in a spy's pocket (receipts, business cards, boarding passes, etc.) that add authenticity to his/her cover.

Field agents need a cover, a false identity to get them close, shade their visibility, and, if caught, protect their sponsor. It doesn't have to be exotic—in fact the blander, the better—but it should go deeper than a name change or haircut. The difference between a successful cover and a burial shroud might be the pocketed ticket stub for a play performance on the night the president's safe was cracked or knowing that bullfights in Portugal are bloodless.

Even a good agent can be undone by a bad cover. Antonio Mendez, the former chief of disguise for the CIA, likens having a cover to being an actor playing a role—but with tougher consequences than any critic's review. He should know: He was awarded the CIA's Intelligence Star of Valor for his role in one of the most successful cover operations of the past half a century.

In 1979, when Iranian militants stormed the American embassy in Teheran, taking scores of hostages, six American diplomats managed to escape to the Canadian embassy. Mendez, with the help of a Hollywood

Mendez's other great exfiltration occurred ten years later in Moscow, during a performance of the Bolshoi Ballet. To aid the defection of a Soviet working for the KGB, along with his wife and child, Mendez and a team that included his own wife, Jonna, used four couples (three of them followed by KGB agents) to switch identities, clothes, and jewelry inside a bathroom during the final act. The identity switch allowed the Soviet to leave the theater undetected. Before fleeing the country, however, the Soviet agent provided immediate payback. He led a CIA operative down a manhole to a cavern below the Kremlin where an interception device could be attached to a communication cable carrying encrypted Soviet messages.

"When he comes to the Great Game, he must go alone . . . at the peril of his head. Then, if he spits, or sits down, or sneezes other than as the people do whom he watches, he may be slain."—Rudyard Kipling, Kim

JOSEPH D. STAFFORD

KATHLEEN F. STAFFORD

HENRY LEE SCHATZ

MERCI CANADA

THANKS CANADA

Six American diplomats escaped Iran in disguise with the help of Mendez.

British spy Robert Baden-Powell, founder of the Boy Scouts, used his natural artistic talent as a cover during World War I. Baden-Powell roamed the Dalmatian coast sketching butterflies whose wing patterns showed the location and design of fortifications as well as gun placements. In case he was caught trespassing, he always carried a bottle of brandy, which he could blame for his confusion.

artist who'd worked on *Planet of the Apes*, helped devise a plan for getting them out. He set up a fake movie company, borrowed a script, and placed ads in Hollywood trade papers announcing the upcoming filming of that movie in Iran. When he flew into Teheran, he had credentials and cover stories for each of the Americans—art director, cameraman, production manager, script consultant, writer, and business manager. Mendez appointed himself director and spent three days rehearsing his cast before leading them through Teheran to the airport and safety.

Modern covers and disguises are, when possible, elaborately detailed. An espionage team might scan death notices of infants from thirty-year-old newspapers, obtain those birth certificates, and then identify schools and workplaces that no longer exist, making background checks nearly impossible. The agents themselves might visit or live in those "hometowns" before undertaking the assignment. As for disguises, the transformation of a twenty-five-year-old into a one-armed septuagenarian is routine magic.

Such a valuable supporting cast was not often available to undercover agents in the past. When English king Alfred the Great wanted to learn the strength of the invading Danish army, he assumed the role of a bard and strolled through their camp singing.

Basic disguise tools such as spirit gum, cold cream, hair dye, false mustaches and a heel insert to change one's walk are part of this CIA-issued disguise kit.

Sir Paul Dukes, the head of Britain's secret service, escaped from Russia after the 1917 Revolution by assuming four separate identities: an agent of the Russian secret police, a Red Army soldier, a man with a crippled leg, and finally a bearded intellectual with a bad cough.

But for creative reach, Dukes was bested by Sarah Emma Edmonds, a Canadian woman who supported the Union side in the Civil War. She disguised herself as an Irish woman, a black slave, and a soldier and actually fought in the battles of Antietam and Fredericksburg. Edmonds was the first woman to receive a pension from the U.S. Army.

Terrorist Ilich Ramirez Sanchez, aka Carlos the Jackal, was adept at targeting men of his age and weight, then stealing their passports and replacing their photos and signatures with his own.

Not all covers are equal, a lesson personified by the American Revolutionary spy Nathan Hale. An unusually tall man with a distinct facial scar, Hale was not built to blend into the background, especially when that background was behind British lines. His cover as a schoolteacher fell apart when the only notes the British found were those hidden in his boots. While he provided no intelligence to George Washington, he did give the United States one of its more memorable quotes: "I only regret that I have one life to give for my country."

Sarah Emma Edmonds, disguised as a solider.

Not all blown covers are entirely the fault of the agent. In the early 1900s two Japanese spies posted to a shipping company in Russia not only learned to speak the language but also studied such minutiae as the rites of the Russian Orthodox Church. To deepen their cover, one of the agents became engaged to a Russian woman. Despite all this effort, the Japanese were arrested on evidence provided by the fiancée, herself a Russian spy.

John Wilkes Booth, the man who assassinated President Abraham Lincoln, was a Confederate synpathizer who used his natural cover as an actor to put himself in position to carry out the killing. Booth, one of the most popular actors of his time and passionately Confederate, had smug

John Wilkes Booth

Though the Civil War ended on April 9, Booth was determined to carry out the assassination. Booth knew Ford's Theatre as well as anyone, having performed in eight plays there, including one—*The Marble Heart*—seen earlier by President Lincoln, who sent a message backstage asking to meet the actor. Booth refused.

Though a bodyguard was supposed to be sitting outside the door to the presidential box, Booth was apparently depending upon his celebrity to gain entry. But the guard, a DC policeman, had left the theater to have a drink at a nearby saloon. Booth walked in and shot the president in the head at approximately 10 PM. Lincoln died the following morning. Booth was hunted down, shot and killed twelve days later in a Virginia barn.

MASTER SPIES

As a fighter pilot in World War I, William Stephenson downed twenty-six German planes, escaped from an enemy POW camp, and made his way back to his squadron, slowing only to take note along the way of German troop placements. In World War II, working as a British agent and spymaster, the Canadian native delivered to President Franklin Roosevelt the map of a scheme to divide Central and South America into German colonies. Between those two wars Stephenson won the world lightweight boxing championship, set a world air-speed record, and became a millionaire with his inventions in radio and electronics.

Stephenson might be the perfect embodiment of the spy as portrayed in movies and books—an agent who can fly his way in and fight his way out while carrying the world's secrets in his back pocket.

But agents' achievements are often measured by more than one yardstick. Defectors who are vilified by the country they betray may have streets named after them in the nations they secretly served.

From the Soviet Union's perspective, **Ronald Pelton** was a great intelligence asset. A communications specialist with the U.S. National Security Agency, Pelton had a photographic memory and fourteen years' worth of secrets to sell in the 1980s. All the Soviet Union needed to do was turn on a tape recorder and ask questions. A U.S. judge saw Pelton in a different light and sentenced him to three concurrent life sentences.

The West, in turn, benefited from Soviet GRU Colonel **Oleg Penkovsky**, who served as an agent in-place for U.S. and British intelligence. A senior officer with Soviet military intelligence, Penkovsky claimed to be motivated by a fear of Soviet nuclear power. But he also admitted frustration with his own lack of advancement, which he blamed on the KGB discovery that his father had fought against the Bolsheviks during the Russian Revolution. Whatever his motivation, Penkovsky had a world of information to share about Soviet missile technology, its network of secret agents around the world, intelligence codes, and the country's military intentions. From 1961

"Intelligence played a tremendous role in keeping the world from the brink, from turning the Cold War into a hot war."—Oleg Kalugin, KGB Major General, retired

Penkovsky's most valuable intelligence came during the Cuban missile crisis. He not only knew the strengths of the intercontinental ballistic missiles the Soviets were hoping to install in Cuba but, more important, knew their limitations as well. Penkovsky's information convinced President John F. Kennedy that Nikita Khrushchev was bluffing, allowing Kennedy to safely call that bluff.

At one point when Thorpe heard what she feared might be a watchman coming toward them, she quickly took off her clothes. The watchmen threw open the door, shined his flashlight on the naked Thorpe, then backed out, apologizing profusely as he went.

through 1962 Penkovsky passed so many classified documents to the CIA, the agency hired a few dozen clerks to file and review them all. His cooperation with the West was discovered by KGB investigators and he was speedily tried and executed. Penkovsky's story is told in the book that earned him the identity of "The Spy Who Saved the World."

She spied in Washington, DC, Poland, Spain, France, and Chile. And if she couldn't get enemy secrets using her considerable charm and intelligence, **Amy Elizabeth Thorpe**, code name: CYNTHIA, had no qualms about using her body. "Ashamed? Not in the least," the American-born Thorpe told her biographer. "My superiors told me that the results of my work saved thousands of British and American lives. . . . Wars are not won by respectable methods."

At the age of eighteen, with bright green eyes and auburn hair, she married thirty-seven-year-old Arthur Peck, the second secretary at the British embassy, and went with him to an assignment in Spain, where she got her first taste of espionage. She helped soldiers on both sides in the Spanish Civil War.

In Poland, where her husband next served in the British embassy, she was recruited by British intelligence to cultivate highly placed Polish sources. Her work resulted in the collection of documents revealing Hitler's plan to partition off Czechoslovakia and information on the work Polish cryptographers were doing to crack Germany's first Enigma enciphering machines.

But her greatest coup came in Washington where, posing as an American journalist, she began an affair with the press attaché at the French embassy. Soon she was delivering to the British cables, files . . . just about anything she asked the attaché to provide. Then she asked the impossible: the Vichy French naval ciphers.

The attaché got the night watchman at the embassy to let him use the back room for a tryst. After a few failed attempts, they drugged the watchman and his dog, let in a safecracker, and made off with the ciphers.

After her husband died, Thorpe married the French press attaché, and they lived out their lives in a castle on a mountain in France.

Elyeza Bazna was a successful spy who depended more upon opportunity than any intelligence training. As valet to the British ambassador to Turkey during World War II, Bazna, code name: CICERO, was lucky enough to work for a man who kept top-secret documents lying about his residence. For documents that were locked in the safe, Cicero knew where the ambassador kept the key. He delivered to the Germans information about Allied bombing plans, the code word for the D-Day invasion (OVERLORD), and details of strategy sessions between President Roosevelt and Prime

Minister Winston Churchill. But the Germans refused to believe that a servant had access to that level of intelligence and did not act upon it.

Richard Sorge was a devoted Soviet Communist who traveled to Germany during World War II to penetrate the Nazi party. The son of a German mining engineer, he was fluent in English, German, French, Russian, Chinese, and Japanese. As complicated as he was, he projected for himself the cover of a congenial pleasure seeker, interested more in parties than politics.

He cultivated a friendship with the German military attaché in Tokyo, who did not speak Japanese. Sorge was only too happy to help his new friend translate (and secretly send to the USSR) sensitive Japanese material.

Long before Sorge gave up his life to aid the Russian Revolution, another agent sacrificed his own trying to crush it. **Sidney Reilly**, known as the Ace of Spies, was an agent for Great Britain during the First World War. Although reputed to be a highly skilled intelligence agent, his appeal today has as much to do with his colorful background as any intelligence operations he performed. At various times he claimed to be a Russian, the son of a Jewish physician from Vienna, or the son of an Irish sea captain. Where he was born, in what year, and under which name were equally murky. He did say he'd been given a British passport by British officers whose lives he'd saved in South America.

Reilly posed as a Russian intelligence officer in Moscow, promising his British handlers that he had an army of more than fifty thousand Russians and Latvians ready to fight the Bolsheviks as soon as the order was issued. No army ever materialized. Before he was captured and killed by the Stalin in 1925, Reilly wrote: "I had been within an ace of becoming master of Russia."

CICERO was paid £300,000 British by the Germans, but most of it was counterfeit money. He was sent to prison for trying to spend it.

As a result of Sorge's intelligence that Japan would not invade the USSR Soviet troops were freed from eastern positions to defend Moscow against the German siege. Years later, Sorge gained a measure of immortality after his execution by the Japanese. In 1964, the Kremlin declared him a Hero of the Soviet Union and a year later put his face on a postage stamp.

They don't wear trench coats or hide their eyes beneath wide-brimmed fedoras, and what murder they commit is often as symbolic as the Philistine agent Delilah's shearing of Samson's hair. But in every important respect, women have shown no shyness in the art of spying and have willingly risked the same fate as men upon exposure. What few remember about **Mata Hari**, the most renowned and perhaps least successful female spy in history, is that she ended up in front of a French firing squad during World War I.

Rose O'Neal Greenhow was luckier, but only because she had friends in very high places. During the Civil War, the Washington, DC, hostess and passionate southern supporter hosted dinners that included future president James Buchanan, Secretary of State William Seward, and nearly every member of Washington's diplomatic corps.

In July 1861 Greenhow passed to Confederate general P. G. T. Beauregard a Union battle plan that showed which route the northern army planned for its campaign in the South. Beauregard quickly deployed troops and artillery at a particularly vulnerable spot along the way. Both Beauregard and Jefferson Davis later credited Greenhow for the devastating Union defeat at the first battle of Bull Run.

When Greenhow was unmasked, she was placed under house arrest and later sent to prison. In both places she continued to smuggle out encoded messages, once by switching shoes with a visitor and another time by sewing a message into the sole of her daughter's shoe.

Because of her friends and her own notoriety (police found love letters in her bedroom from Senator Henry Wilson of Massachusetts, chairman of the Senate Military Affairs Committee), Greenhow was spared execution and only exiled to Richmond. She later went to Europe, where she published a memoir, lobbied for the Confederate cause, and was presented to Queen Victoria and Emperor Napoleon III. A year later, attempting to sneak back into America, her ship ran aground and she drowned. Greenhow was buried with full military honors by the Confederacy.

The Union had its own embedded spy during the Civil War in **Elizabeth Van Lew**. Her neighbors called her Mad Bet, not because she raved on the streets of Richmond but for her unimaginable betrayal of her aristocratic class. She not only publicly opposed slavery but also freed her own.

Van Lew had a secret room in her house where she hid Union spies and prisoners of war, including young Lieutenant Paul Revere, grandson of the Revolutionary nightrider. Although her house was often searched by suspicious Confederate agents, the room was never discovered. Van Lew actively gathered information by visiting Union soldiers in Richmond hospitals where, after inquiring for their health, she'd grill them for knowledge of the size and location of enemy troops. She

Another of Van Lew's accomplishments was the placement of one of her former slaves, Mary Bowser, as a domestic in the house of Confederate president Jefferson Davis. Although Bowser feigned illiteracy, she not only could read and write but also possessed a near-perfect photographic memory, which she applied to the letters and documents she found on Davis's desk.

Oposite page: Mata Hari, perhaps the best known and least successful female spy; top: Mrs. Greenhow and her daughter imprisoned in the Old Capitol, Washington.

passed that information to General Ulysses Grant by way of a five-station relay she'd created.

Van Lew was later appointed postmistress of Richmond by General Grant. Bowser was posthumously (1995) inducted into the U.S. Army Intelligence Hall of Fame.

Another disparate pair of Civil War spies is worth mentioning for the peril they endured while practicing their honorable treachery. **Belle Boyd** was another southerner who passed intelligence to the Confederacy and, like Rose Greenhow, later wrote a memoir that was celebrated in Europe. Boyd once shot a Yankee soldier for trying to put a Union flag on her house. During a battle near her home in Virginia, she raced across an open field under heavy fire to warn Confederate troops of the Union army's plan to trap them. Boyd was beguiling enough that when a Union navy vessel captured the ship spiriting her to England, she persuaded the Union captain not only to let her go but also to marry her.

Harriet Tubman was equally fearless while working for the northern cause. An escaped slave, she made eighteen trips along the Underground Railroad and brought out three hundred slaves, including her brother and parents. Called Moses by the slaves she helped, she's said to have never lost one along the way to freedom, which may be due to the fact that she carried a gun and threatened to shoot any who tried to turn back. At one point the Confederates offered a reward of $40,000 for her capture.

In 1863 she guided a contingent of Union troops up the Combahee River in South Carolina, where nearly eight hundred slaves were freed and a ton of Confederate supplies destroyed. At her death in 1913, Tubman was accorded a full military funeral.

Unlike their Civil War spy sisters, Martha Dodd and Elizabeth Bentley were drawn to espionage not by patriotism but by more intimate passions. **Martha Dodd**, the daughter of the U.S. ambassador to Germany in the 1930s, was young, beautiful, and more than a little wild. She came to hate the Nazi regime in Berlin and was easily recruited to espionage work by her Russian lover, diplomat

Above: Belle Boyd, Confederate spy dressed in Confederate uniform.

Opposite page: Harriet Tubman, who ferried 300 slaves to freedom.

After her father retired, Dodd became a full-time Soviet spy. But her desire to marry Ninogradov was blocked by both Ninogradov and his handlers, in no small part because of Dodd's other love affairs and her inability to keep quiet about her strong Communist beliefs, a bad trait in an undercover agent. Still, the Soviets retained her until 1949. By that time she'd married an American millionaire and recruited not only him but also her brother to the cause. The family left the United States to live in Cuba and finally in Czechoslovakia, where Dodd died in 1990.

Boris Ninogradov. Dodd copied documents in her father's safe and reported any embassy conversation that might help Russia check the growing Nazi threat.

Elizabeth Bentley's American ancestors arrived with the *Mayflower* and fought in the Revolutionary War; one of them, Roger Sherman, signed the Declaration of Independence. Quite a pedigree for a woman who became known in America as the "Red Spy Queen."

Bentley, a Vassar graduate, was working as a librarian and teacher in New York when she met and fell in love with Soviet NKVD officer Jacob Golos. In 1938 he recruited her to work as his secretary and act as courier for his Soviet intelligence network. When Golos died in 1944, Bentley fell in love with the married FBI agent who convinced her to turn against the Soviets.

Elizabeth Bentley, "Red Spy Queen."

Venona

In an oblique way, Senator McCarthy's claims were verified in 1995 when thousands of decrypted Soviet communications, collected and analyzed over a period of forty years, were finally made public. The messages, which dealt with Soviet diplomatic concerns and all manner of espionage, indicated that 349 individuals in the United States had a "covert relationship" with the Soviet Union.

Among those identified were the State Department's Alger Hiss; economist Harry Dexter White, who was one of the founders of the International Monetary Fund; American physicist Ted Hall, who leaked a detailed description of the plutonium bomb Fat Man to the Soviets; German physicist Klaus Fuchs, who worked on the Manhattan Project; and Julius and Ethel Rosenberg, who were executed as spies in 1953.

Of the hundreds of thousands of intercepted messages, three thousand were partially or completely decrypted. Varied analysis techniques were employed, and some luck was involved as well. Cipher pads, the sheets of paper used to create a particular cipher, were supposed to be used only one time. However, they were sometimes used multiple times by Soviet cryptologists. Defectors also provided useful information. And there have been rumors that embassies were bugged in order to listen to the clicks of the encryption machines.

The Venona papers can be viewed at the National Security Agency's National Cryptologic Museum at Fort Meade, Maryland, or online at www.nsa.gov/venona/.

While Senator McCarthy was proved right about the great number of Red spies in the United States, his accusations against individuals were not supported by any evidence. Of the 349 individuals mentioned in the Venona papers, fewer than half have been identified.

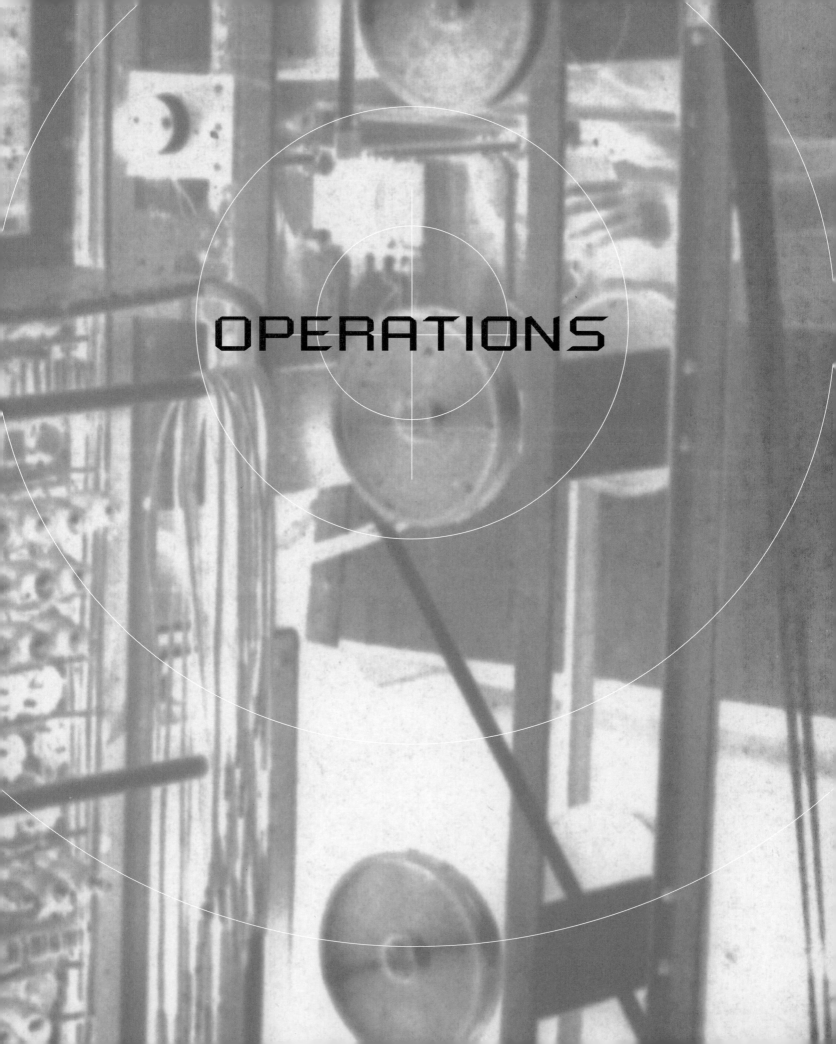

OPERATIONS

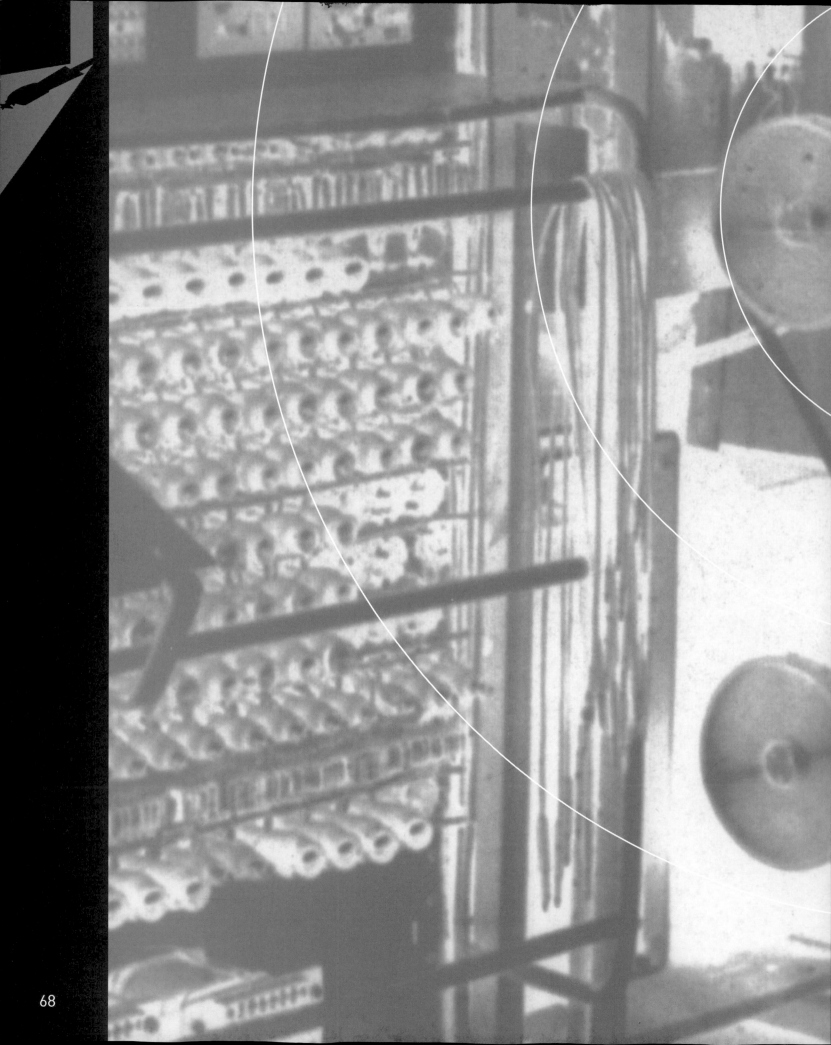

Most major intelligence operations depend on some mixture of deceit, courage, and surprise. And because each additional agent increases the risk of exposure, it helps to have some luck as well. When it works, however—when an operation of many moving parts achieves its purpose—the rewards can be far greater as well.

The Italian Job

The Central Intelligence Agency's first major covert (that is, secret) action designed to influence events, was to fix an Italian election. Italy's Communist and Socialist parties had joined forces in 1948 and seemed sure to win control of the government. But President Harry Truman was determined not to let Communism take over a Western nation (even if it wasn't his) and aimed his year-old agency at Europe's boot.

With $10 million in payoffs and some dirty tricks (form letters sent from Italian immigrants in America read, "If the forces of true democracy should lose in the Italian election . . . we won't send any more money to you, our relatives"), the CIA turned the election upside down. The crowning blow came to the Communist and Socialist parties when a newspaper published an allegedly "top secret" Communist policy paper known as the Zorin Plan, which called for the elimination of all priests who refused to swear fealty to the godless Communist state. Catholics everywhere were outraged.

"They come not single spies, but in battalions."—*William Shakespeare*, Hamlet

ZIMMERMANN TELEGRAM

During the bleakest period of World War I, British intelligence intercepted a German telegram with the potential to change the course of the war. Unlike the normal challenge of making a forged document appear real, the British had a genuine telegram that looked too good to be true.

The year was 1917, and British, French and German armies were at a stalemate, neither side able to pass beyond a line of trenches stretching from Belgium to Italy. That situation threatened to change as Germany readied to launch two hundred submarines. Great Britain could not continue to fight without control of the sea.

The German strategy was to sink all ships, including those of neutral countries such as the United States, which sent a great deal of ammunition and other goods to England. President Woodrow Wilson had resisted all efforts to pull the United States into the war, despite repeated acts of sabotage by German agents on American soil. But as a hedge, Germany sought Mexico as a partner if the United States did finally enter the war. The offer, outlined in the intercepted telegram from Germany's Secretary of State Arthur Zimmermann, promised Mexico all its lost territories, including Texas, for its military help.

As explosive as the telegram was, William "Blinker" Hall, the director of British naval intelligence, held it for a full month. He knew the Americans would suspect a forgery and also feared letting the Germans know their top-secret cipher code had been broken.

Eventually Hall was able to find a copy of the Zimmermann telegram sent by Western Union using a less sophisticated cipher. Hall gave U.S. intelligence the original and enough "keys" to decipher it themselves. Eventually, Wilson declared war, and the Germans never knew their code was broken.

> To disguise the role played by British agents in the telegram's intercept, Hall maneuvered the British press into writing stories about the superiority of American intelligence.

Zimmermann telegraph, coded and uncoded.

WESTERN UNION
TELEGRAM

NEWCOMB CARLTON, PRES.

115	3528
0247	11518
392	10371
8276	18101
1589	87893
17166	13
4991	7382
970	5454
3638	18222
21604	4797
5905	13347
2262	1340
6992	8784
9559	22464
3092	16127
11347	1714
3670	

BERNST...

TELEGRAM RECEIVED.

...ter 1-8-58
...rson, State Dept.

By _Mark A Eckdorf Archivist_
Date _Oct 22, 1931_

FROM 2nd from London # 5747.

"We intend to begin on the first of February
unrestricted submarine warfare. We shall endeavor
in spite of this to keep the United States of
America neutral. In the event of this not succeeding, we make Mexico a proposal of alliance on the
following basis: make war together, make peace
together, generous financial support and an under-
standing on our part that Mexico is to reconquer
the lost territory in Texas, New Mexico, and
Arizona. The settlement in detail is left to you.
You will inform the President of the above most
secretly as soon as the outbreak of war with the
United States of America is certain and add the
suggestion that he should, on his own initiative,
~~invite~~ Japan to immediate adherence and at the same
time mediate between Japan and ourselves. Please
call the President's attention to the fact that
the ruthless employment of our submarines now
offers the prospect of compelling England in a
few months to make peace." Signed, ZIMMERMANN.

The pigeons were parachuted behind enemy lines, two to a crate, with a message inside the cage asking anyone who found the birds to attach a message about German troop strength and location to the birds' legs, then let them out of their cages to fly back to England. What the Germans were supposed to notice, and did, was that all the birds were dropped in the area of Calais.

Four British soldiers shoulder a rubber Sherman tank.

D-Day

One of the great military deceptions in history depended on inflatable tanks, invisible airfields, hundreds of homing pigeons parachuted into enemy territory, and a double agent known as GARBO.

Operation OVERLORD was designed to fool the Germans into thinking the Allies would invade Europe near the French city of Calais rather than Normandy. Spreading Germany's artillery and troops was crucial to a successful landing on exposed beaches.

Because Calais was closer to England and the best guess of many German leaders, including Hitler, the Allies worked to reinforce that notion. They built fake airfields (rendering the real ones invisible) and broadcast the sounds of airplane engines throughout the night. Across the channel from Calais, the Allies constructed huge camps that contained thousands of inflatable rubber tanks, trucks, gun tractors, and landing craft. When German spy planes flew overhead to take photographs, gunners on the ground were ordered to fire wide.

Inflatable decoy landing barge used in Operation OVERLORD.

Convoy of dummy barges, designed to fool German air reconnaisance.

German agents controlled by England reported that (nonexistent) Allied armies in Scotland and England were preparing invasions of Norway and Calais. Misinformation was printed in bogus editions of real magazines. False rumors were intentionally spread among Allied troops and underground supporters in Europe. An actor (a British soldier spotted at a talent show) impersonated Field Marshal Bernard "Monty" Montgomery in appearances that lent weight to the Calais option.

The most valuable agent in Operation OVERLORD was a Spaniard, Juan Pujol Garcia, code name: GARBO. Pujol, who'd fought in the Spanish Civil War, was both anti-Nazi and anti-Communist. He went to the British embassy in Madrid at the start of the war to volunteer his services as a spy for England, but was turned down. In order to make himself appear more attractive to the British, he persuaded the German ABWEHR intelligence service to send him to England, where he would spy for them. The Germans agreed, little realizing that Pujol's visa was a forgery. That didn't stop him, though. He went to a library in Lisbon and researched enough of England to make his reports seem factual. In the first of many inventions, Pujol created three subagents who traveled with him on his imaginary trips through England, getting into and out of jams.

When he tried to volunteer again, an American navy lieutenant recommended him to British intelligence, and Pujol began his service as a double agent—GARBO (so named because of his acting ability) to the British, ARABEL to the Germans. He sent fabricated intelligence to Germany supplied to him by twenty-five agents he'd invented. Not only did he give each of these agents covers and detailed personal histories, but he developed a different writing style for each of their reports as well. (Germany sent him $340,000 by the end of the war to pay these nonexistent agents.) GARBO greatly impressed his German handlers by predicting the North African invasion, though by design the information arrived too late to be of any use.

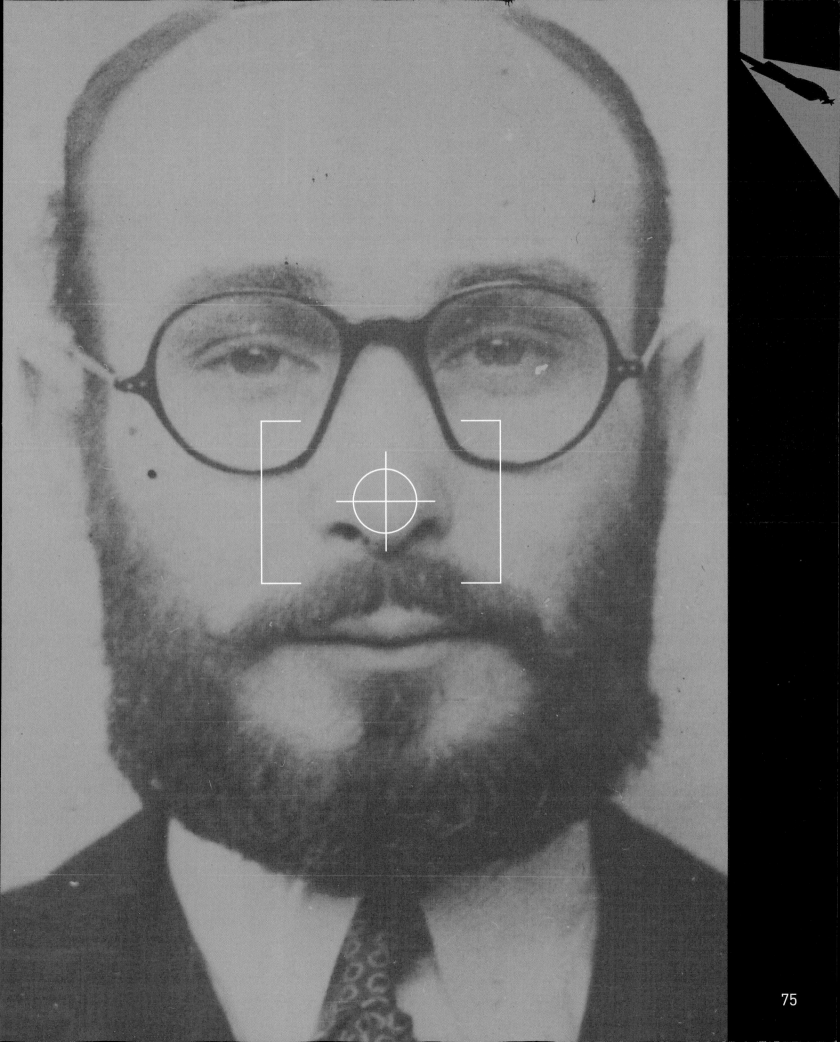

Corpse of Major Martin being taken by submarine to the Mediterranean; opposite page: Soldiers sending and receiving messages with the Enigma machine during World War II.

When the Allies landed on Normandy (again he sent a quite accurate but hours-late report of the attack), GARBO convinced German intelligence that it was a false feint and the real attack would still come at Calais. Three weeks later, nineteen infantry and two artillery divisions were still at Calais looking for an invasion that had already occurred elsewhere.

Another successful use of a double agent involved a program known as XX (for "double-cross")—a committee of amateur and professional spies who managed to trip up Germany. It centered on a double agent by the name of Arthur Owens, whom the Germans believed was working for them. The XX committee used Owens to get in touch with other German agents in England and turn them. As a result, the XX committee was able to send an enormous amount of false information to German intelligence.

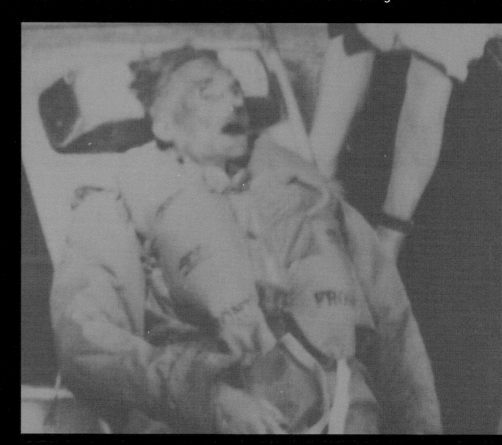

Enigma

Germany's Enigma was a cipher machine that looked like a manual type-writer with a few extra layers of rotors and letter disks. But it was sophisticated enough to create an almost limitless number of cipher possibilities, and just portable enough to be taken onto battlefields and submarines. Germany's unshakable confidence in Enigma allowed the Allies time to un-

The World War II battle to break Enigma was fought not in trenches or on the high seas but in a Victorian estate north of London with the most eccentric army ever assembled. Bletchley Park became home to linguists, writers, history professors, puzzle experts, and cryptanalysts under a military command that had to throw its ideas about discipline out the window (British novelist Angus Wilson was known to run naked around the swan pool).

Polish cryptanalysts had the first success at deciphering Enigma messages, but as the machines became more complex, they turned to France for help. When Germany invaded both countries, those Polish and French agents escaped to England, bringing their information and expertise to Bletchley Park.

The work at Bletchley Park was credited with shortening the war by at least two years. With decoded intercepts, the Allies helped ships avoid submarines as well as predict the time and vicinity of German air strikes and the intention and location of the German army. Allied plans for D-Day and the invasions of Italy and North Africa were greatly aided by the million deciphered intercepts from Enigma.

One of the remarkable achievements at Bletchley Park was that secret work there was never leaked. By the end of the war there were more than ten

Bletchley Park codebreakers taking a break on the lawn.

When the war ended, the Bletchley Park staff swore an oath of secrecy. Incredibly, that oath was kept for thirty years until the publication in 1974 of a book about Enigma called *The Ultra Secret* by F.W. Winterbotham.

thousand people involved with Enigma and other code breaking, most of them female clerks. Winston Churchill personally congratulated those clerks, whom he called his "Geese that laid the golden egg and never cackled."

Alan Turing, a British cryptologist and mathematician, was one of the geniuses at the center of Bletchley Park, as well as one of its eccentrics. He sometimes wore a gas mask to combat hay fever, chained his coffee cup to a radiator, and was known to run the forty miles from Bletchley Park to meetings in London wearing an alarm clock tied to his waist. Only twenty-four, Turing built the first machine at Bletchley, called the Bronze Goddess, which successfully decrypted some of the early Enigma ciphers in 1940.

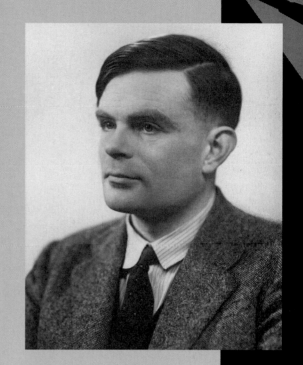

Right: British cryptologist and mathematician, Alan Turing; below: Women codebreakers at Bletchley Park operating Colossus computer.

Red Army Down

Successful operations sometimes come with a cost in lives. There can be other, less predictable repercussions as well, such as the blowback from an operation against an adversary that returns uninvited to harm its creator. The CIA's role in the defeat of the Soviet Union in Afghanistan in the 1980s is an example of a much celebrated operation with consequences that have yet to be fully measured. But embers of the September 11 tragedy were certainly carried on its wind.

After the 1979 invasion of Afghanistan by the Soviet Union, the CIA began equipping Afghan fighters with WWI rifles and other armaments at a cost of $5 million a year. But the scope of that covert operation increased dramatically when a Texas congressman named Charlie Wilson and an out-of-favor CIA agent Gus Avrokotos (a.k.a. Dr. Dirty) became convinced that with enough money and planning, the Soviet Union could actually be defeated.

As detailed in George Crile's book *Charlie Wilson's War*, the CIA was initially a reluctant partner. Content to let the Afghans inflict minor wounds

At the same time that a Democratic Congress refused to give President Ronald Reagan $19 million to fund the Nicaraguan Contras, Wilson was getting so much congressional money that he threatened to "flood" the CIA with dollars. Ironically Wilson benefited from Reagan's Contra troubles, telling his Democratic colleagues that by giving money to the Afghans, they would insulate themselves from Republican charges that they were soft on Communism.

Afghani resistance fighters.

on the Soviet giant, this sudden effort by Wilson and Avrokotos to actually try and win the war seemed both ludicrous and dangerous. An escalation of that kind might provoke the Soviets to invade Pakistan (an ally of the Mujahideen), and from there it was one short step to Saudi Arabia and its oil. But Wilson was relentless. And because of his position on the Defense Appropriations Subcommittee, which controlled the CIA's budget, he was in a position to pressure the agency into growing the annual budget for the Afghanistan operation from $5 million to $750 million by the end of the 1980s.

On the face of it, Congressman Wilson would appear to be the wrong man to be involved any intelligence operation. Six-foot-six-inches tall in cowboy boots and bearing a passing resemblance to Rock Hudson, he was never out of the spotlight and, more often than not, that light revealed Wilson partying in hot tubs with Miss America contestants or drunkenly crashing his car. The stories of Wilson showing up in conservative Muslim countries with tall blondes in revealing outfits were legendary.

Inspired by their hatred of Communism, the pair brokered deals between Pakistan and Israel and commissioned the Chinese to develop weapons. By their own admission they broke enough laws and agency regulations to have any other pair burned at the stake. But neither the White House nor the State Department ever vetoed their plans, because Wilson built enough political protection to skip the step of submitting them for approval.

At the same time that a Democratic Congress refused to give President Ronald Reagan $19 million to fund the Nicaraguan Contras, Wilson was getting so much congressional money that he threatened to "flood" the CIA with dollars. Ironically Wilson benefited from Reagan's Contra troubles, telling his Democratic colleagues that by giving money to the Afghans, they would insulate themselves from Republican charges that they were soft on Communism.

In February 1989, when the last Russian soldier retreated from Afghanistan, there were some in the intelligence community who feared the consequences that might result from having armed an Afghan fundamentalist army. The victory gave the entire Arab world, including those interested in darker aims, a great lift. Then there were all of the stinger missiles that the CIA tried to buy back with little success. Some of those same Afghan military commanders would later support Saddam Hussein in the first Gulf War and join forces with Osama bin Laden and al Qaeda.

One of the Mujahideen that the CIA supported, Gulbuddin Hekmatyar, was accused by other Afghanis of being a fanatic who killed moderate Muslims and threw acid in the face of women he considered improperly dressed. After September 11 the CIA tried and failed to assassinate him with a satellite guided missile.

10.

GREAT SPY
FAILURES

No intelligence agency is immune to failure. Israel, for example, now considered to have one of the world's most effective intelligence networks, in 1954 recruited Jewish Egyptians to blow up British and American facilities in Cairo and Alexandria, hoping Egyptian insurgents would be blamed. The plot was revealed, but only after a U.S. diplomatic facility and a movie theater were destroyed.

The U.S. intelligence services, while enjoying great successes, have had their failures as well. The Japanese attack on Pearl Harbor in 1941 may rank as one of the worst because of feuding among intelligence services that failed to keep Pearl Harbor military authorities fully informed. There was also the accusation that FBI director J. Edgar Hoover disregarded crucial information because he disliked the messenger who delivered it.

The Japanese developed a cipher known as Purple, to protect its communications. The cipher had been broken by U.S. Navy intelligence more than a year before Pearl Harbor, but those decrypted messages were fiercely protected. Often only a summary of the messages—and not every one—was shared. So when the War Department sent army commander Lieutenant General Walter Short in Hawaii a warning two weeks before Pearl Harbor of "hostile action possible at any moment," he interpreted that to mean local Japanese might try to sabotage his planes. His response was to park them as close together as possible. In that formation, one Japanese bomb could take out half a dozen planes. More troubling was the lack of response to a navy intelligence message sent to Admiral Husband E. Kimmel, the Pearl Harbor fleet commander just days before the attack, that read, "This dispatch is to be considered a war warning" and "an aggressive move by Japan is expected within the next few days." The admiral did not raise any alarms. On that Sunday morning, in fact, anti-aircraft guns were unmanned and most sailors were ashore.

"Why, with some of the finest intelligence available in our history, with the almost certain knowledge that war was at hand . . . was it possible for a Pearl Harbor to occur?"—*Postwar U.S. congressional committee hearings.*

More than twenty-four hundred Americans were killed during that Sunday-morning bombing of Pearl Harbor in 1941, and another eleven hundred were wounded. Two battleships, the *Arizona* and the *Oklahoma*, were sunk; eight others were badly damaged, along with three cruisers and three destroyers. On land, more than 350 fighter planes were destroyed. And if the Japanese had decided to hit a huge gasoline storage facility, the entire Pacific fleet might have been forced to retreat twenty-five hundred miles to America's West Coast.

Double agent Dusko Popov and his wife.

Professional jealousy between army and navy intelligence concerning which would monitor messages from Japan led to a sloppy compromise. Each service took turns—odd days for one, even days for the other. As a result, crucial messages were missed or ignored. And each agency assumed the other was passing those intercepts to military officials who never received them.

Maybe the most troubling intelligence failure involved FBI director J. Edgar Hoover and double agent Dusko Popov. Recruited to spy for Germany, the Yugoslavian immediately volunteered his services to the British. Four months before Pearl Harbor, he came to the United States with evidence of the planned attack. When shown the evidence (contained in a microdot), however, Hoover did not pass it along to military intelligence. He also refused to allow Popov to maintain his credibility with the Germans by going to Pearl Harbor. Hoover dismissed Popov as a "Slavic playboy" because of his reputation as a notorious womanizer. Popov's reponse to Hoover was, "I don't think a choirboy could do my job."

The Pearl Harbor failure did contribute to positive results five months later. Navy intelligence, mindful of its earlier missed opportunity, scored a major coup by intercepting and interpreting messages that led to the decisive victory at Midway and the death of the commander in chief of the Japanese fleet. It was the first defeat of the Japanese navy in more than three hundred years and is considered the turning point of the war in the Pacific.

Burning and damaged ships at Pearl Harbor.

Dutch Disaster

A missed warning in a radio signal during World War II led to a needless loss of lives and the dismantling of an important intelligence operation in the Netherlands. After Germany invaded their country, Dutch resistance members set up transmitting stations to send military intelligence to Great Britain. Germans located one of those stations in 1941 using radio directional finders loaded on the back of moving trucks.

When the Germans forced the radio operator to send a false message to Great Britain, he intentionally omitted a phrase that every message was supposed to contain. This omission should have immediately signaled that the operator had been compromised. The British receiver had another chance to see what was happening after the operator managed to sneak the word *caught* into his next message, but the British receiver at the other end missed both of these cues.

The Germans sent continued requests for weapons, ammunition, money, and personnel. But, as each new agent arrived from England, the Germans were waiting to snatch both the agent and his radio, which was used by the Germans to lure more agents and weaponry. The operation, known as NORDPOL, went undetected for nearly two years. By war's end, dozens of agents had been executed as a result of the lapse by that first radio operator.

Czech Reprisal

An operation carried out by the British Special Operations Executive (SOE) in World War II had extreme repercussions. The SOE was created in response to the war to do the dirty work of sabotage and assassination behind enemy lines. Its successes, particularly in the jungles of Burma, are legendary.

But one operation in Czechoslovakia provoked particularly deadly consequences for unarmed citizens. The SOE parachuted two Czech agents and a few radio operators and cipher clerks behind enemy lines to assassinate the head of Germany's Gestapo, Reinhard Heydrich, also known as the "blond beast" for his cruelty. Information used to track him was provided by a maid, who took his itinerary from a trash can and gave it to SOE agents.

Heydrich was ambushed and killed in his car. Reprisals for that assassination included the killing of more than four thousand Czechs, including every man, woman, and child who lived in Lidice, the Czech village where the SOE agents landed. The village itself was completely razed.

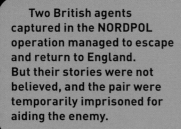

Two British agents captured in the NORDPOL operation managed to escape and return to England. But their stories were not believed, and the pair were temporarily imprisoned for aiding the enemy.

The SOE had a reputation for being, as one critic called it, "a collection of talented roughnecks, activists, saboteurs and murderers." It was an organization that didn't tolerate quitters (the SOE's motto was "Once in, never out"). Recruits who failed to qualify or tried to resign were confined for the duration of the war in a special detention center at Inverlair Lodge in Inverness-shire, Scotland, without any contact with friends or family. That center became the model for the popular British television show *The Prisoner.*

Bay of Pigs

It was doomed from the start—a bad idea, hampered by poor tactics and questionable intelligence. As covert operations go, the CIA-sponsored invasion of Cuba in 1961 was the trifecta of failure with consequences that might have led to a nuclear war eighteen months later. Espionage students may never find a more instructive fiasco to dissect.

Start with the concept: Fourteen hundred Cuban exiles are trained by the CIA to invade a country with an army of two hundred thousand and hope to overthrow its government. To make things more difficult, the sponsoring country, the United States, insists on deniability, which means it will provide neither air support nor rescue if things go wrong. But the CIA insists that these obstacles will be overcome when the Cuban people rise up as one to overthrow Fidel Castro once the invasion begins.

The intelligence supporting this view came not from penetration agents but from Cuban exiles living in Miami who, like Iraqi exiles forty-five years later, swore the people were eagerly waiting for liberators to arrive. Senior intelligence analysts with the CIA were extremely skeptical, but they were kept out of the invasion planning, which was run by the operations side of CIA.

The tactics of the operation were questionable as well. The original landing site for the invasion was in an area near mountains where a small group of anti-Castro Cubans could provide cover. But after reporters in *The New York Times* and Latin American newspapers quoted Miami Cubans who bragged about CIA training camps and the great invasion soon to come, that site was switched to a "quieter" location—a remote beach, separated from the mountains by a swamp and a fifty-mile hike.

When the rebels landed there, after midnight on April 17, Cuban troops were not far away, having been alerted by Soviet intelligence. The next disappointment was the sinking of a supply ship carrying ten days' worth of supplies and ammunition.

The fighting was over within days, but not before the President Kennedy swore there was no U.S. involvement in the invasion. One hundred fourteen Cuban invaders were killed, and 1,189 were taken prisoner. Although Americans were forbidden to participate in the operation, four CIA officers died flying planes after Cuban trainees balked at the last minute.

Before the Bay of Pigs, another team of anti-Castro rebels landed in Cuba hoping to provoke an uprising. Not only did locals refuse to fight, but they also withheld food and water and helped Castro's forces track the men down.

Eight CIA planes bombed Cuban airfields two days before the invasion. A ninth plane, painted with Cuban air force markings and strategically pocked with bullet holes, flew to Miami. The pilot, who claimed to be with the Cuban air force, said he'd bombed the Cuban airfields before defecting.

Cuban Missile Crisis

It must have looked like a winning hand to Soviet premier Nikita Khrushchev. Eighteen months after the Bay of Pigs debacle, with Cuba swimming in sympathy after a sovereign nation had attacked without provocation, Khrushchev warned President Kennedy that his country would go to any length to protect its Cuban friends. What he didn't tell Kennedy was that his protection plan included the installation of nuclear missiles.

Kennedy, having already suffered through the Bay of Pigs, the erection of the Berlin Wall, and the Soviet Union's resumption of atmospheric nuclear tests during the first two years of his administration, was reluctant to provoke another crisis with the Soviets.

As for Fidel Castro, his justifiable fear that the United States was not done with its attempts to overthrow him led to his acceptance of a Soviet missile plan that risked annihilation for himself and Cuba.

The crisis began in October 1962 with aerial photographs of missile sites under construction in Cuba. The evidence that the sites were of the kind the Soviet Union built for its nuclear arsenal came from an American intelligence analyst. It was then that the U.S. defector in place, Russian colonel Oleg Penkovsky, had information that convinced the CIA and President Kennedy that the Soviet Union did not have the missile capability to wage a war with the United States.

While the missiles themselves never got closer than two hundred miles to Cuba, the twelve-day stalemate between Kennedy and Khrushchev terrified the world.

In the end it was Penkovsky's information that emboldened Kennedy to stay tough until Khrushchev backed down—sending the president this message, "Only lunatics or suicides who themselves want to perish would seek to destroy our country." Kennedy then offered a face-saving compromise. If Khrushchev would turn back the ship carrying the missiles, the United States would not invade Cuba. Khrushchev's failure was Kennedy's triumph, and it reinvigorated his presidencey.

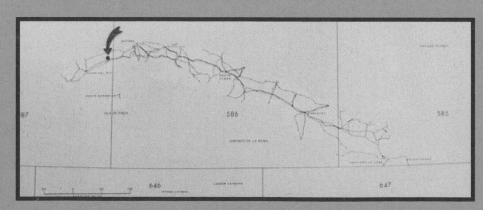

Cuban missile crisis, and aerial view of the site.

TRACKED PRIME MOVERS

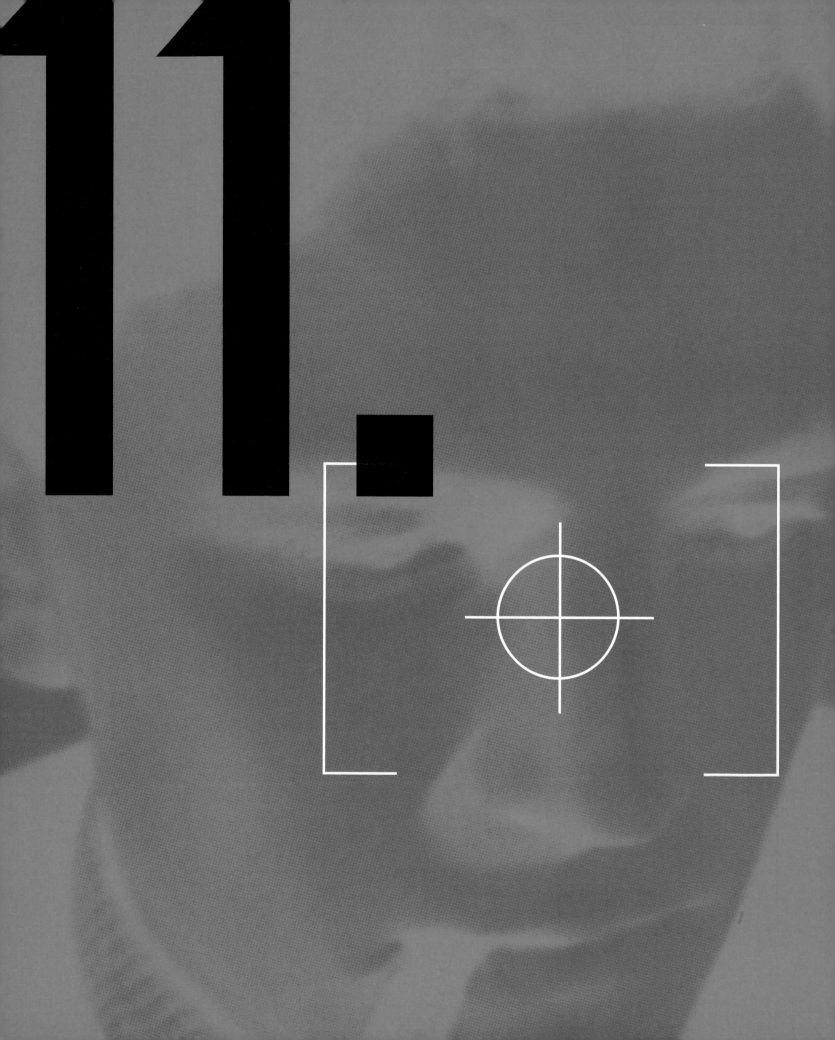

11.

TRAITORS

There would be no glory in betraying their own country. And they certainly didn't do it for the money, since none of the spies ever expected to be paid. To the question of what motivated the Cambridge spy ring, a collection of upper-class British intellectuals recruited to spy for the Soviet Union and Communism in the 1930s, the answer seems to be twofold—disgust for the social, political, and economic systems of their time, and a belief, naive as it might have been, that the Soviet Union represented something fine, a real chance to build a society where all people actually were equal.

"We repudiated entirely customary morals, conventions, and traditional wisdom," said economist John Maynard Keynes, a member of the Cambridge University Apostles Club, from which three of the five spies were recruited. "[We] recognized no moral obligation on us, no inner sanction, to conform or obey."

The Cambridge spies stand in stark contrast to modern-day turncoats, whose motives seem rather small and cheap. The CIA's Aldrich Ames sold out for money—to pay debts, straighten his teeth, buy his new wife a half-million-dollar home and himself some $500 Italian shoes. Robert Hanssen, his ego as bruised as old fruit, was obsessed with showing the FBI he was smarter and more clever than all those others promoted ahead of him. As for John Walker, a U.S. Navy Warrant Officer who recruited his son and brother and tried to persuade his own daughter to have an abortion so she might stay in the Army and join his spy team (he called her an "idiot" when she refused), no motive seems worth the print.

"As a spy who turned his family in . . . I don't care. —Convicted atomic spy David Greenglass on 60 Minutes II, December 5, 2001

Clockwise from upper left: Robert Hanssen, the most dangerous spy in FBI history; Kim Philby, Cambridge spy; John Walker's electronic gear, used to find hidden listening devices; convicted spy, John Walker who claimed,

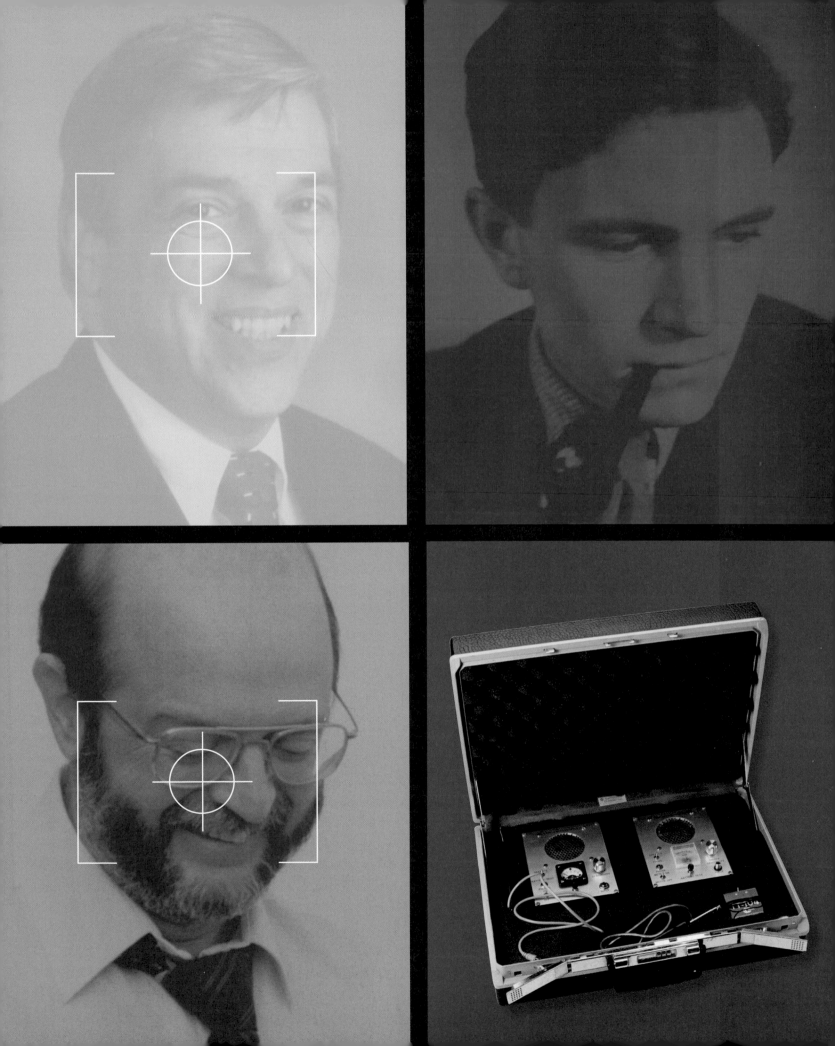

After his recruitment, Philby went to Spain in 1937 as a newspaper correspondent to write about the Spanish Civil War. To establish his credentials as a right-winger, he wrote biased stories in favor of Franco's Fascists. (Franco himself awarded Philby a medal for his reporting.) When he returned to England, Philby was hired by British intelligence.

Blunt used young agents employed by Britain's MI5 to seduce the couriers carrying those embassy pouches. He'd make two copies of any important documents, one for England and one for Russia.

In 1945 Russian defector Konstantin Volkov contacted British authorities to offer information about two moles in the British Foreign Office, including one who was head of a counterintelligence branch in London. That offer of information was sent to England, where it was received by Kim Philby, one of the moles Volkov intended to expose. Volkov disappeared without a trace.

Philby admitted his role while being interviewed in Beirut. He promised to tell all at the next session, but slipped out of Lebanon on a Soviet freighter. He died in Moscow in 1988, buried with the honor accorded a KGB general.

Harold "Kim" Philby, the most successful of the Cambridge spies, personified the type of recruit the Soviets sought. A member of a well-connected family with a father who'd been knighted, he had the social status necessary to rise in class-conscious Britain and the "correct" political sympathies. As Philby saw it, the Depression was further proof that capitalism only widened the gulf between rich and poor. The only hope for stemming the rise of fascism in Germany and Spain, which certainly threatened the world, was the young experiment known as Communism. His recruiter, who may have been a professor at Cambridge, emphasized that he was not being asked to spy *against* England but *for* the Soviet Union, to save it from Hitler's boot.

Philby was a Soviet agent for thirty years. During that time he rose in rank to head the Soviet section of British intelligence and was at one time in line to become head of all British intelligence. He was privy to a treasure trove of government secrets, both British and American. And he had a number of Cambridge schoolmates as accomplices.

Anthony Blunt, the son of an Anglican minister, recruited Soviet agents while betraying British ones. His entry-level position in British intelligence gave him access to the mail pouches of neutral embassies, which provided a great deal of intelligence for the USSR.

Donald Maclean, the son of a British cabinet minister and another Cambridge spy, became head of the Foreign Office's American department, where he gathered information on the American atomic weapons program and British/American strategies to halt the Soviet Union's spreading influence. When asked what Maclean's motives were, KGB general Oleg Kalugin, who managed Maclean in the Soviet Union, answered, "Ideology."

Guy Burgess and John Cairncross operated with impunity for decades. It was not because there were no signs of a mole; rather, it was because no one in British intelligence wanted to believe that any of their colleagues would betray class and country. In addition, when an incriminating report did reach the highest levels, a member of the spy ring would often be the one to receive it.

The spy ring was exposed a few members at a time over the course of years. The first break came in 1951 when an FBI counterintelligence agent discovered that someone had used a telegraph in the British embassy in Washington, DC, to send messages to Moscow. By the time it was traced to Donald Maclean, he and Guy Burgess had been warned by Kim Philby and escaped to the Soviet Union.

The departure of Burgess, who had lived with Kim Philby's family while in Washington, cast enough suspicion on him that he lost his top-secret clearance. But the British did not have enough on Philby to force a confession until 1963, twelve years later.

Atomic Spy Ring

If Britain was embarrassed by its Cambridge spy ring, the United States fared no better during its Manhattan Project, a program to develop an atomic bomb. The program, with operational sites in England and Canada, was primarily located in Los Alamos, New Mexico, where hundreds of the world's best scientists were brought together. While Germany and Japan were aware of efforts to create what Albert Einstein described to U.S. president Roosevelt as "extremely powerful bombs of a new type," it appears that nearly all of the intelligence leaks benefited the Soviet Union, a World War II ally working furiously to build its own nuclear bomb.

The U.S. Army, in charge of security at Los Alamos, insisted that notes and documents be locked in safes each night. Guards checked ID badges, and the site was enclosed by fences. But far less concern was given to the political sympathies of the scientists recruited for the job. There were too few brilliant scientists available to exclude any because of ideology.

The most active and valuable spy at Los Alamos was German-born physicist Klaus Fuchs. He gave the Soviet Union calculations on half a dozen steps in the separation of isotopes of uranium and other aspects of the bomb's production. By all accounts Fuchs was also one of the most talented and valuable members of the Manhattan team.

None of the atomic spies was exposed until 1950, when decryption of Soviet messages in the Venona program led to Fuchs. Once intelligence authorities persuaded him to confess, others fell like dominoes.

Fuchs led to Harry Gold who led to David Greenglass, a U.S. Army corporal and machinist assigned to Los Alamos who gave the Soviets information about the facility as well as sketches of Fat Man the bomb dropped on Nagasaki in 1945.

In exchange for a reduction in his sentence, Greenglass gave evidence against his sister Ethel Rosenberg and her husband, Julius. The Rosenbergs, members of the Communist party, vehemently denied being spies. Their case drew worldwide attention and protest, especially after they were both sentenced to die. They were executed in the electric chair at Sing Sing Prison in New York, leaving behind two young children.

The world reaction to those executions was intense and emotional. John Early Haynes and Harvey Klehr, authors of the book *Venona: Decoding Soviet Espionage in America*, write that U.S. authorities did not intend to carry out the executions, expecting the death sentences to pressure Julius to confess. And David Greenglass, in an Associated Press story in December 2001, said he lied about his sister Ethel Rosenberg's involvement to keep his wife, Ruth, out of prison and to reduce his own sentence.

Among other scientists identified as spies was Italian physicist Bruno Pontecorvo. When the FBI found evidence in his home that he was a mem-

The head of the nuclear laboratory at Los Alamos was J. Robert Oppenheimer. His wife, brother, and various friends had been Communist party members, and Oppenheimer himself had contributed money to left-wing causes. But there is no evidence that he betrayed any atomic secrets.

Fuchs took his spy craft seriously. Here is his routine for meeting his regular courier, Harry Gold: On the first and third Saturday of each month at exactly 4 PM he would stand on a street corner in New York City holding a green book and tennis ball. When Gold, wearing a pair of gloves and holding another glove, approached and asked the way to Chinatown, Fuchs would confirm contact by saying, "Chinatown is closed at 5 PM. This was the secret code that indicated that the meeting was safe. If anything about the code varied, Fuchs would know to abort the meeting."

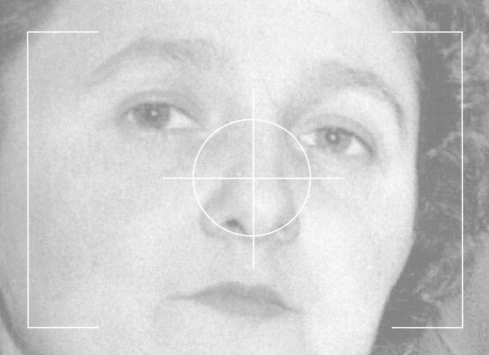

ber of the Communist party, it sent a message to the MI6 representative in Washington, DC. That representative was the Cambridge spy Kim Philby. He warned Pontecorvo in time for him to escape to the Soviet Union. American physicist Ted Hall, who was eighteen when he worked at Los Alamos, admitted in a 1996 interview that he gave nuclear information to the Soviet Union because he "worried about the dangers of an American monopoly of atomic weapons."

A wire screen separates Ethel and Julius Rosenberg during transport to prison after their conviction as traitors.

Some scientists have since stated that the work of the atomic spies did nothing worse than speed the Soviet Union's atomic development by a year or two. The scientific principles were already well known, and the Soviets had their own talented team of physicists at work on the project. More damage, they say, was done to U.S. national pride. But two years is strong leverage in the balance of power.

In 1947 CIA head Allen Dulles told a U.S. congressional committee that his agency would be the first to know if another country had developed a nuclear weapon. The CIA and President Truman later predicted the Soviet Union would not be capable of that technological feat until the mid-1950s at the earliest. When the Soviets detonated their first nuclear weapon in 1949, Truman initially maintained it had to be a nuclear "accident."

During their trial much of the evidence against the Rosenbergs was withheld to prevent the Soviet Union from discovering that its secret code had been broken. But later evidence seemed conclusive as to their guilt. In *Khrushchev Remembers: The Glasnost Tapes* the former Soviet premier said, "I cannot specifically say what kind of help they gave us, but I heard from . . . Stalin . . . that the Rosenbergs provided very significant help in accelerating the production of our atomic bomb."

Roy Howard may not have been afraid of Communism, but Western intelligence agencies certainly were. From the first spark of revolution in 1917 to its explosion after World War II, those spy shops feared that the Soviet Union's aggressive form of Marxism might torch the entire world. They were wrong, of course—it only torched about half the world.

Without ever meeting on a battlefield, the Soviet Union and Western nations fought through surrogates in Korea, Vietnam, Africa and Afghanistan. Between wars there was nonstop engagement of a different kind in back alleys, bedrooms, and intelligence agencies themselves. And there was little professional courtesy in any of it.

When the Cold War began in 1947, Western intelligence agencies found themselves at a distinct disadvantage. Many, if not all, of these agencies had been penetrated by the Soviet Union, which hadn't trusted its World War II allies any more than its German and Japanese enemies.

The United States had just created its CIA, however, it was immediately handicapped by the fact that the other American intelligence groups—the Army, Navy, State Department, or FBI—were reluctant and slow to open their books to the new kid. Hoover's FBI for example, so resented having to hand over intelligence collection in Latin America that when this responsibility was redelegated to the CIA, the FBI left some offices completely bare, having removed all the case files.

The Soviet Union in the meantime was sending out scores of agents, much like settlers in a land rush—and with similar results. Czechoslovakia, Poland, and Albania all fell under Soviet control. When British and American intelligence sent trained Albanian exiles into that country to foment a revolt, the results were disastrous. It is estimated that five hundred Albanians agents died between 1949 and 1953, most as a result of intelligence leaks by Soviet moles. The few Albanian agents who managed to avoid capture for a number of weeks saw no evidence that their countrymen were ready to take up arms.

"The menace of Bolshevism in the United States is about as great as the menace of sunstroke in Greenland or chilblains in the Sahara."
—Roy Howard, chairman of Scripps Howard Newspapers in the 1930s

The West did have its successes, including an ambitious British operation in Vienna, which was jointly occupied by the Soviet Union, England, France, and the United States after World War II. Unable to intercept Soviet communications, the British decided to tap into underground telephone cables linked to the Russian occupation headquarters. They bought a building seventy feet from the underground lines, dug a tunnel, and, to account for all the people coming and going, set up a store in the building that sold British tweeds. The tap worked from 1951 to 1955, when the occupation forces returned control of Vienna to Austria. The clothing store was just as successful, which was problematic for the spies, who had to stock and sell the suddenly popular tweeds.

In 1946, the Soviets scored their own eavesdropping coup by placing a sophisticated listening device inside a carved wooden version of the Great Seal of the United States, which Russian school children presented to the U.S. ambassador. It hung in his Moscow study until technicians discovered it six years later. In 1960 an outraged Ambassador Henry Cabot Lodge, Jr. revealed it at the United Nations—where some admired it for its ingenuity.

The CIA had to hit the ground running, and its batting average those first years was predictably low. The agency failed to foresee a Communist coup in Czechoslovakia, the Israeli victory over its neighboring Arab states, the Berlin blockade, or the Soviet Union's first nuclear bomb.

Ambassdor Henry Cabot Lodge, Jr. points out details of the bugged Great Seal.

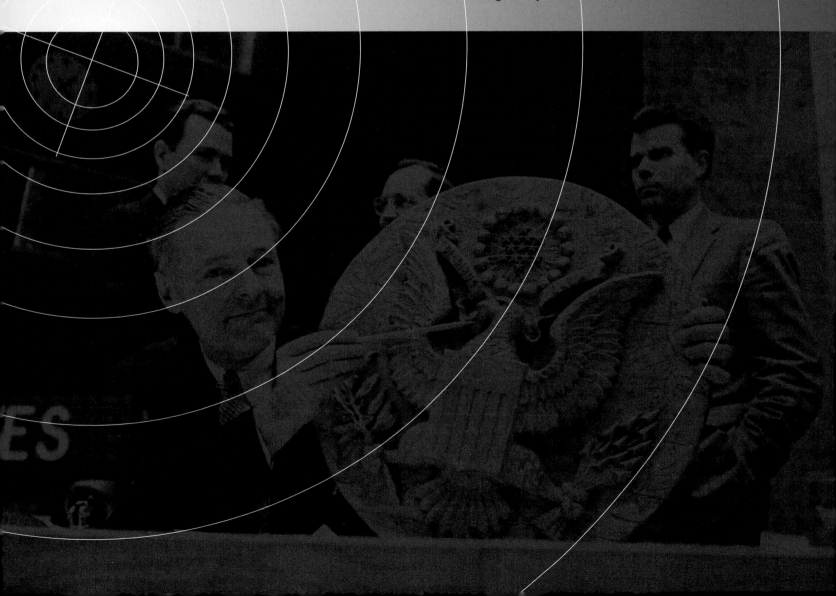

Neither side was shy about using sex to achieve its ends, though the Soviet Union was the more accomplished. In 1960 the British secretary of state for war, John D. Profumo, was set up by a Soviet agent with a teenage prostitute. The resulting Profumo Affair cost both Profumo and British prime minister Harold Macmillan their jobs.

Canada's Royal Canadian Mounted Police once tried its hand at dirty tricks in an operation code-named Deep Root by photographing the wife of a Soviet diplomat in bed with a Canadian man. But when they tried to blackmail her, she got on the next plane to the Soviet Union.

If the Soviet Union was better at infiltrating human agents, the West was far more successful in attracting defectors. After the initial infatuation with Communism in the 1920s and '30s, the flow of sympathizers switched from East to West. One of the first was Igor Gouzenko, a cipher clerk in the Soviet embassy in Ottawa, Canada. When the Soviet Union ordered him to return home, he and his wife decided the West was best and defected with their son. Gouzenko provided documents that identified atomic spy scientist Alan Nunn May and two moles, both with the code name Elli. One Elli, an embassy clerk, was arrested. The other Elli was thought to be Kim Philby.

As noted earlier, intelligence agencies are extremely cautious with defectors, knowing how much damage can be done by disinformation or the suspicion of it. An example of that mayhem played out in the early 1960s, when two Soviet agents defected to the United States.

The first to switch sides was KGB officer Anatoly Golytsin, who provided the CIA with a list of spies and a shocking pronouncement: Every Western intelligence agency had been penetrated by Soviet agents, some embedded at the highest levels.

While Western agencies were chewing on that, another defector, Yuri Nosenko—the deputy chief of the KGB's Seventh Department—knocked on the door with information that undermined some of Golytsin's claims. Golytsin insisted that Nosenko had been sent by the Soviet Union to discredit him, and he convinced a very powerful supporter: the CIA's head of counterintelligence, James Jesus Angleton.

Angleton had been shocked to learn of the extent of the Cambridge spy operation in England, especially the treachery of his British counterpart Kim Philby. If it could happen there, he reasoned, why not in America? But while Angleton was championing Golytsin, FBI director J. Edgar Hoover had pinned his colors to another Soviet informant, a diplomat known only by the code name FEDORA, who did not defect but stayed in place. In the stalemate that followed, Angleton undertook a mole hunt that lasted into the early 1970s and paralyzed parts of the CIA. As a result of what was later

The mole hunt in England led to the investigation of the two top officers in MI5 and jumped from there to a suspicion that British premier Harold Wilson might have been a Russian spy.

Another bugging device found in the American Embassy in Moscow.

called "the monster plot," a number of CIA officers were investigated and some careers came to a halt. When he failed to rid the Soviet bloc division of four CIA officers he suspected, Angleton quarantined that division from any sensitive case files. Following leads provided by Golytsin, even U.S. ambassador Averell Harriman was suspected for a time of being a Soviet spy.

Not all double agents are quite so damaging. Take Boris Morros, the owner of a bankrupt record company and a small-time Hollywood producer. The Russian-born Morros said the Soviet Union threatened to kill his parents while on a visit to Leningrad if he didn't spy for them in America. Morros had agreed, convincing the Soviets that he had accessed top-rate intelligence from his friends in high places, including the pope and the president of the United States. Although technically a spy for the Soviet Union, he apparently never gave them anything beyond the script for a musical he wanted money to produce—*Autumn for Stalin and Motherland* (shades of *The Producers*!).

In 1947 Morros went to the FBI and confessed. He agreed to work for the bureau and in 1957 testified against some of the spies he'd worked with. In 1955 he wrote a book, *My Ten Years as a Counter-Spy.*

As tension mounted between East and West, so too did spy operations and recriminations. Between 1970 and 1985 Britain expelled 144 Soviets under diplomatic cover. The Soviets answered tit for tat, expelling not only genuine spies but also businessmen and journalists. Then there were the spy swaps. When the Soviets didn't have a Western spy to swap, they were not above taking a "hostage" to swap instead.

The continuous news stories of spy networks and their nefarious deeds led to a Red hysteria. There seemed no limit to what intelligence agencies would do to counter Communism, from a harebrained British proposal to smuggle millions of moths into the Soviet Union in the hope they'd gobble up all the country's movie screens and prevent the showing of propaganda, to U.S. intelligence agencies' violation of its citizens' rights.

Senate investigations reported that from 1942 to 1968 the FBI conducted at least two hundred unlawful break-ins and a thousand unauthorized telephone taps. In 1956 an operation known as COINTELPRO (COunter INTELligenc PROgram) was launched. The goal of this secret FBI program was to discredit, disrupt, and destroy radical groups. To neutralize these targets the FBI wire tapped phones, leaked false information, forged correspondence, searched homes, and sent anonymous letters to group members' parents and friends.

Peter and Helen Kroger, a.k.a. Morris and Leontina Cohen.

In 1965 a young British man, Gerald Brooke, carried anti-Communist pamphlets into the Soviet Union. He was sentenced to fifteen years in prison, but after serving four was swapped for Morris Cohen and his wife, Leontina, who'd run a spy ring using as a cover a London bookshop that specialized in books on torture and sadomasochism.

13.

BERLIN:
CITY OF SPIES

victorious Allied powers that strode into that desolation recognized Berlin as precious territory.

Berlin's primary value was neither its gold nor its art treasures but its symbolic location at the center of communications and transportation routes that radiated like wheel spokes throughout Europe. More important, because the city was a hundred miles inside Soviet-controlled territory, its intelligence value to the United States, Great Britain, France, and the Soviet Union, which collectively ruled the city, was immeasurable.

Berlin provided the perfect perch from which the West could spy on the Soviets inside the bear's own lair. For Russia, West Berlin was a provocation, the equivalent of an espionage dart jabbed into its backside. The city's importance to both sides can be measured by the tenacity of the spy battles waged there from 1947 until 1989, when the wall came down. Two years later the Soviet Union had dissolved. It is a period of Berlin's history that can be read as chapters in a good spy novel.

The Blockade

If winning German hearts and minds was ever a goal of the Soviet Union, it certainly wasn't in the thoughts of the first Soviet soldiers to occupy Berlin. After battling a brutal German invasion of Russia for four years, culminating in the siege of Stalingrad where half a million Red Army troops died and at least that many Russian civilians, the soldiers who entered Berlin took revenge by wide-spread looting, killing, and raping.

By the time the American, British, and French armies arrived two months later, Berlin had been sacked of its art treasures and more than 75 percent of its industrial capacity.

The military commanders who had jurisdiction over the western half of Berlin were initially optimistic about joint cooperation with the Soviets. To that end, America's civilian intelligence officers were ordered to play nice.

The arrival of a new Soviet commander in 1947 changed things dramatically. What started as mild harassment grew into major interference with the flow of people and goods into West Berlin. Tensions rose to such a level that American commander general Lucius Clay warned Washington that warfare might come with "dramatic suddenness." The United States went so far as to develop a war plan (code name: TROJAN) for dropping nuclear bombs on Soviet cities.

Soviet soldiers dismantled the city's electrical generators and entire factories, packing the machinery onto trains bound for the USSR. This grand theft, which crippled one of the Europe's greatest industrial cities, would hurt the Soviets during their long occupation of East Berlin.

demand. Within months, thousands of intelligence agents had swarmed into Berlin, restoring its reputation as a city of spies.

On June 19, 1948, the Soviets halted all train traffic into West Berlin. Four days later, road and ship traffic was stopped and electricity cut to the two million citizens of West Berlin. The West responded three days later by beginning a nearly yearlong airlift called Operation Vittles into the city. Although the Russian air force threatened to interfere with the flights, the only fatal action was the accidental collision of a British airliner with the Soviet war plane that had been harassing it, killing everyone aboard both planes.

At midnight on May 12, 1949, the blockade was lifted and electricity returned to West Berlin. During the eleven months of the blockade the Allied airlift had flown 277,000 flights and delivered 2.5 million tons of food and fuel.

Another Tunnel

In 1951 the Soviets in East Germany began using landlines rather than wireless communications such as telegraphs to send military messages to the Soviet Union. Because these lines were inside Soviet-occupied territory, the West had no access to the vital intelligence they carried. The only hope was to take advantage of West Berlin's location to tap the underground landlines.

Replicating the British tunnel in Vienna, which was code-named PROJECT SILVER, the CIA's Allen Dulles named the Berlin tunnel PROJECT GOLD. The challenge in Berlin would be greater, because the distance to these lines was longer, and the trunk communication line itself six feet deep.

The digging began in February 1954 under a radar site and warehouse that had been constructed to hide the tunnel's source. Dirt was removed in boxes marked as radar gear. It took a full year to complete the five-hundred-yard tunnel, which was fifteen feet below the surface and had six feet of headroom. It was stuffed with all manner of electronic gear, air-conditioning, heating, soundproofing, and a washer and separate dryer. An East German agent had provided information on where to find the tap chamber, a baseball-sized electronic box acting as a switch for the three telephone cables and 172 circuits, each able to carry eighteen channels at a time.

The tap was remarkably successful given that the Soviet Union knew about it before the digging began. George Blake, a British intelligence

There were an estimated eighty agencies and thousands of spies working in Berlin and the two Germanys during the occupation. And it seemed that for every twenty spies there was a writer taking notes for a movie or book.

The Soviets expected that the blockade would create such hunger, and the winter such discomfort, the citizens of West Berlin would demand that Western occupiers leave Berlin during the winter of '49. In their estimation, the snow and ice would make it impossible for the airlift to continue landing planes every ninety seconds as was needed to properly supply the city. But that winter, which became known as the meteorological miracle, was the fairest in memory, and the airlift never slowed.

The original plan, which involved placing a tap on the cable under a canal, failed when two West German agents who were using a battery-operated toy boat to drag a tap line were caught and executed.

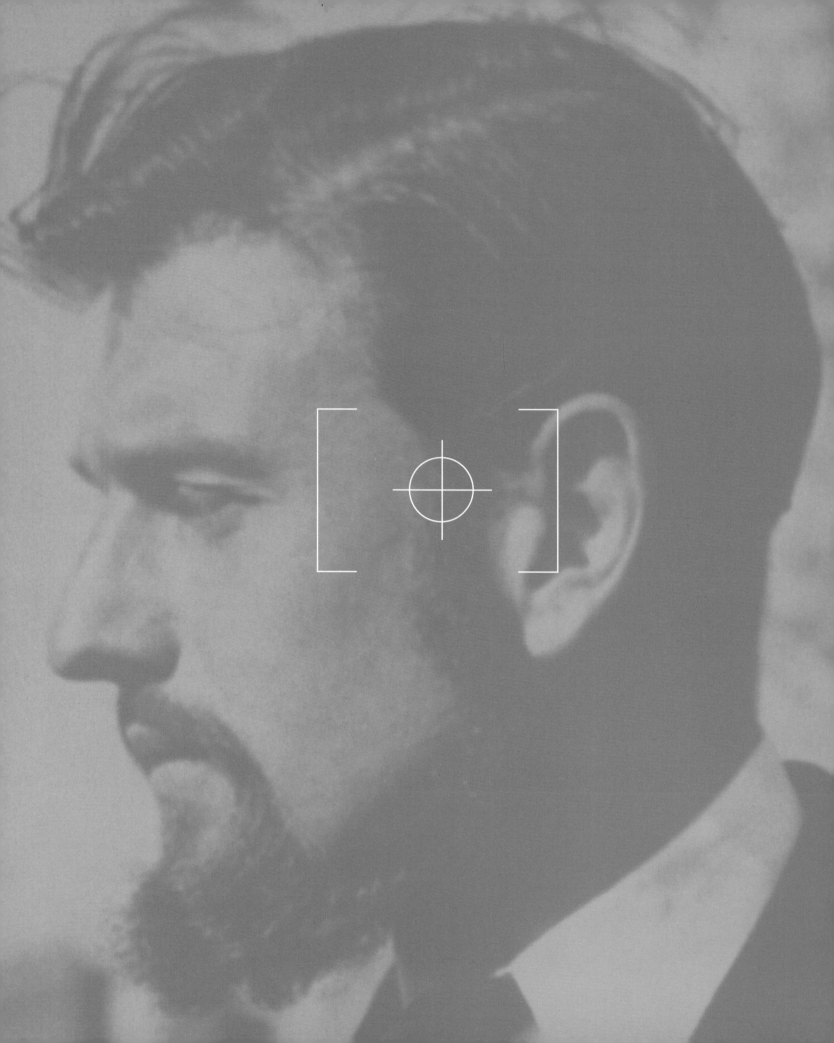

The tunnel was nearly exposed during the first winter storm. A West German agent realized that the snow above the tunnel route was melting as a result of the underground heaters. He was able to warn the diggers to turn the heat off and the coolers on before the East Germans noticed.

Opposite page: George Blake, British intelligence volunteer to the KGB; above: Russian soldier removing insulation from a cable in the Berlin tunnel, after its "accidental" discovery by East German soldiers.

"The leaders of the United States are not such idiots as to fight over Berlin.—*Nikita Khrushchev, Soviet premier during construction of the Berlin Wall*

YOU ARE LEAVING
THE AMERICAN SECTOR
ВЫ ВЫЕЗЖАЕТЕ ИЗ
АМЕРИКАНСКОГО СЕКТОРА
VOUS SORTEZ
DU SECTEUR AMERICAIN
SIE VERLASSEN DEN AMERIKANISCHEN SEKTOR

This rope dangling from a window in East Berlin shows the escape route of a family of five who slid down the rope to safety. The window faces West Berlin.

The Wall

Some sought escape by climbing over it and others by tunneling under neath. Then there were the brave few who launched themselves in hot-air balloons on starless nights. Among those who successfully traversed the Berlin Wall were scuba divers who swam the canals that flowed below it and those who played dead in coffins shipped from East to West. But for every person who succeeded, someone else was caught trying—and many of them died for their efforts.

If Berlin was a metaphor for the Cold War, then the wall was its emblem, the enduring symbol of the battle between freedom and repression. Built in 1961 to keep East Germans from fleeing to the West, it came down twenty-eight years and thousands of spy stories later under sledgehammers wielded by citizens of a soon-to-be reunited Berlin.

For the first sixteen years of Berlin's occupation, residents of East and West were able to walk from one side of the city to the other. East German agents coming to spy in the West could nod to their western counterparts going the other way. The problem with this arrangement for East Germany was that many of its citizens—attracted by West Germany's booming economy or resentful of Soviet and East German control—passed through West Berlin never to come back. From 1949 to 1961, 2.7 million East Germans made their escape, many via Berlin.

To stem the flow the East German government built a six-foot barricade of wood and barbed wire literally overnight on August 13, 1961. The immediate response was a call-up of Western troops and a rush of East Germans hoping to get through the porous sections of the barrier before it could be reinforced. By the end of August more than twenty-five thousand East Germans had passed through the barrier.

⚐ The barrier grew into a white concrete wall thirteen feet high and twenty-seven miles long (another seventy-mile wall was built to separate West Berlin from German territory to the south, west, and north). To prevent the use of grappling hooks, the wall was rounded at the top; it was also fortified with electric wire and land mines and guarded by dogs and armed soldiers in watchtowers.

Among the first to escape were East German police and soldiers, often bringing their weapons with them. Others climbed through drainpipes or swam the Spree. On one Berlin street, apartment buildings were designated East German, while the sidewalk in front of them belonged to the West. Residents climbed out the low windows or jumped from upper stories into bedsheets held by firefighters. The first casualty of the wall was Rudolf Urban, who broke his neck jumping from one of these windows.

Apart from making escape more difficult, the wall thwarted espionage agents on both sides. The tension created by the wall, including a standoff of tanks at Checkpoint Charlie—the official passway to the American sector for non-Germans and diplomats—initially gave intelligence agents a greater role in Berlin. Over time, however, the wall's impermeability diminished Berlin's role as a nexus for espionage activities.

But spying continued, as did escape attempts. People squeezed into tiny spaces within or under automobiles and hid inside suitcases or hollow surfboards. One car made more than a dozen trips, each time carrying a person in the space behind its front grille, before the border guards caught on. A few large trucks crashed through the barriers. The most labor-intensive of the escape methods were the estimated twenty-eight tunnels built under the wall. The most successful of these was built by a West German student named Wolfgang Fuchs and some of his university friends. Fifty-seven people escaped through Fuchs's tunnel, including a three-year-old who thought he'd traveled through hell and was pleased to report there were no wild animals there.

Above: East Berlin workers brick up a wall to prevent escape attempts; left: Once safely across the border, a woman crawls from her hiding place in a modified car.

The most infamous escape attempt was by eighteen-year-old East German Peter Fechter, who was shot while running across Checkpoint Charlie. He lay crying for help for nearly an hour while East German guards let him bleed to death.

The images of Berliners dismantling the wall—taking turns with sledge-hammers, pickaxes, and dull-bladed knives—were broadcast throughout the world. People came from all over Europe to witness the fall of something that had seemed horribly permanent, a wall that separated not only neighbors but families.

Later the grim statistics would sink in. Five thousand forty-three people had successfully escaped from East Berlin, but 260 had died in the attempt.

U.S. Military Police guarding the border at Checkpoint Charlie.

WET WORK

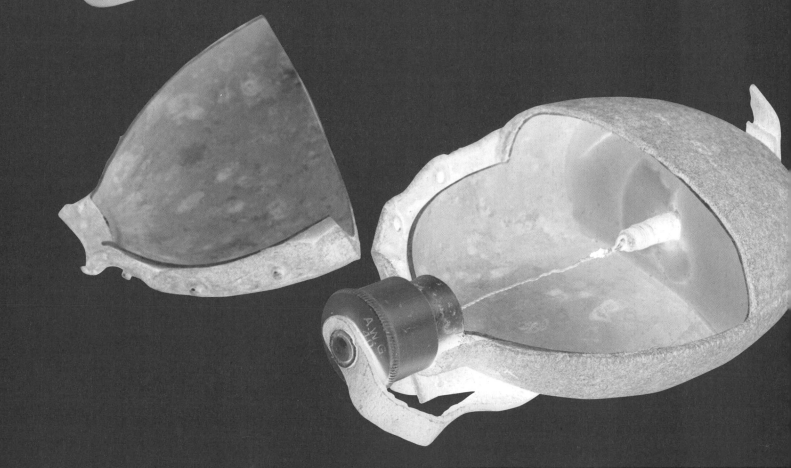

This double-barreled gas gun packed
twice the wallop of the one used to
assassinate Lev Rebet.

The death had to appear natural. No bullet holes, stab wounds, or unsightly garrote marks. Because the target was a well-known anti-Communist living in Germany, the Soviets insisted that the "wet work"—their descriptive term for murder and violence—be untraceable.

A Soviet KGB officer was sent to Munich in spring 1957 to locate and study his victim. In October, he was joined by an armaments expert from Moscow who arrived with a newly designed weapon—a six-inch-long aluminum tube that weighed less than half a pound and fired a spray of potassium cyanide. When inhaled, the gas paralyzed the arteries that carry blood to the brain. Not only would the death appear to be a heart attack, but there would also be no trace of the gas in case of an autopsy.

On the morning of the hit, the Soviet agent was already in the building when his target arrived for work and began to climb the spiral staircase. The agent started down to meet him, his weapon hidden inside a folded newspaper. When the two were a step apart, the agent sprayed the gas into his face then continued out of the building and tossed the weapon into a canal.

The assassination of Ukrainian nationalist and writer Lev Rebet was ruled a heart attack. We know the details of his killing (and a similar one committed by the same Soviet agent a few years later) only because he, Bogdan Stashinskiy, confessed after defecting to the West in 1961.

There has never been a dearth of lethal adventures in the world of espionage. Unlike the intelligence agents of fiction and cinema, however, who dispatch enemy spies by the handful, real intelligence agents tend to follow a golden rule that is mutually beneficial: Why do unto others and risk having them do unto you?

Of course in times of war (and that includes Cold ones), restrictions on the fiendish ways to a kill are lifted. One of the more down-and-dirty cases

SMERSH—a contraction of *Smert Shpionam* ("death to spies") made famous by James Bond novels—was a real organization charged with weeding out spies, going after defectors, interrogating returning Soviet prisoners of war, and executing front-line soldiers accused of spreading "defeatism" in the ranks.

"If the United States is to survive, long standing American concepts of 'fair play' must be reconsidered."—Lieutenant General James Doolittle, 1954 Report of President Eisenhower on CIA Covert Operations

After his arrest, Mercader claimed the murder was an act of jealousy, because Trotsky was having an affair with the American woman only he could love. A sympathetic Mexican court sentenced him to just seventeen years. Upon his release, the Kremlin awarded Mercader the Order of the Soviet Union.

Israel shut down MOSSAD after a Moroccan waiter in Norway was misidentified as Ali Hassan Salameh and killed. The real Salameh, Black September's operations chief, was killed five years later in Beirut.

Less lethal but just as unsuccessful was a plot to harm Cuba's economy by manipulating the price of sugar. The CIA contracted with a London commodities house to force down the price of Cuba's chief export. After spending $1 million on the scheme, the CIA barely affected the market.

of assassination occurred in 1978 after Georgi Markov, a Bulgarian dissident and writer living in Britain, was targeted by the Bulgarian government for his BBC broadcasts about that country's civil rights abuses. When the Bulgarians asked their more experienced friends for help, the Soviet KGB offered three options: a poison jelly to spread on Markov's skin, food poisoning, or a nasty pellet gun. The Bulgarians opted for the pellet gun and were provided with . . . an umbrella, but not the type designed for rain.

One fall day while walking across London's Waterloo Bridge, Markov was bumped by a stranger whose umbrella poked him in the leg. Just before he died, he told doctors about the incident. An autopsy found the poison pellet. Although the discovery was of no use to Markov, it did save the life of another Bulgarian émigré who was gravely ill at the time. Doctors found and removed the ricin pellet from his back.

There are more direct ways to kill a man. Take the assassination of Leon Trotsky, one of the fathers of the Russian Revolution and a much-hated rival of Joseph Stalin. After sending Trotsky into exile, Stalin spent ten years locating him, and finally sent SMERSH agent Ramon Mercader to Mexico in 1940 to kill him.

Mercader, posing as a French journalist, seduced an American woman working with Trotsky to get past his guards. When after months of trying he was granted an interview with Trotsky, Mercader pulled a thirteen-inch ice ax from his coat and sank it in Trotsky's head.

Even the CIA is no stranger to assassination as a tactic—planning several, succeeding at none... But one plan that was never pulled off stands out. As part of an operation known as Mongoose, U.S. intelligence agents during the Kennedy administration plotted a variety of ways to kill Cuba's Fidel Castro.

Among the ideas was one to saturate his cigars with botulism bacilli; another suggested planting explosive seashells on the beach where Castro liked to swim, and providing him with a poison wet suit. Equally "creative" were the ideas to undermine him in the eyes of Cubans. A hallucinogen such as LSD was to be sprayed in his face during a televised speech. Thallium salts, snuck into his boots, might cause Castro's famous beard to fall out. All of these plans were abandoned during the Cuban missile crisis.

Some assassination plans are simpler than others, especially if there's no need to provide escape routes. Two Arab al Qaeda suicide bombers were sent to kill Ahmad Shah Massoud, the leader of Northern Alliance rebels

Fidel Castro holds up a U.S. newspaper with a headline about an assassination plot against him

who opposed the Taliban in Afghanistan. Posing as journalist and photographer, the two men met with Massoud two days before September 11. All three were killed when a bomb inside the camera detonated.

There will never be a full reckoning of "natural" deaths that were actually caused by clever assassins. Even the assassinations we know of are sometimes muddied as to their motives and sponsorship. Amid the conspiracy theories surrounding the assassination of John F. Kennedy is one that claims Lee Harvey Oswald was hired to kill Kennedy by the Soviet KGB.

We do know of at least one foiled assassination, because the man who was both assassin and foiler refused to get wet. Captain Nikolay Khokhlov, a Soviet wet work specialist, was ordered to assassinate Georgi Okolovich, the Russian-born head of an anti-Soviet group in West Germany. Khokhlov

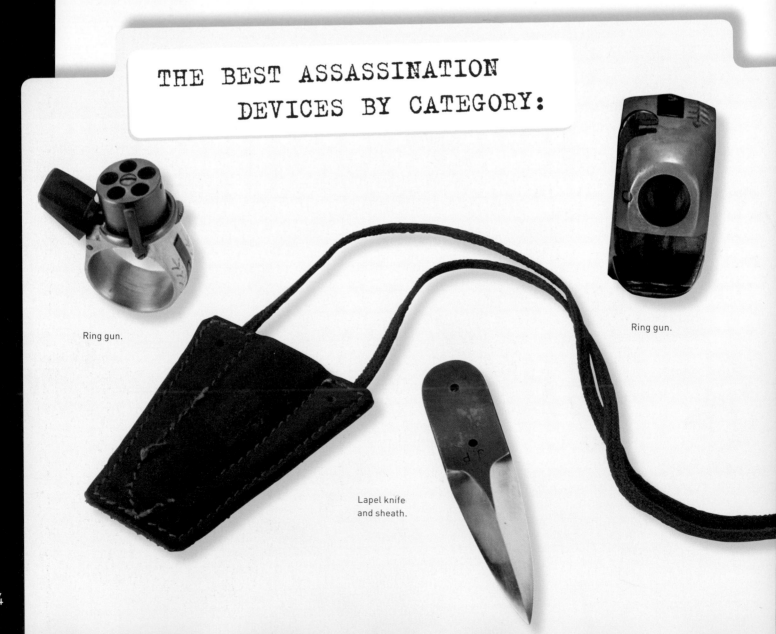

THE BEST ASSASSINATION DEVICES BY CATEGORY:

Ring gun.

Ring gun.

Lapel knife and sheath.

was given an electric gun that fired cyanide-tipped bullets hidden within a gold cigarette case. He proceeded to Okolovich's apartment—but only to warn him of the plot.

Khokhlov's change of heart was influenced by his wife's religious beliefs. The born-again assassin, realizing there would be no hosannas awaiting him in the Soviet Union, defected with his wife to West Berlin just one day before the wall separating the two Berlins was erected.

Khokhlov did not come empty-handed. He brought Soviet operational intelligence and three assassination devices that might have come from an Ian Fleming novel. Two of the weapons were disguised as cigarette cases while the other looked like a miniature pistol. All three were exceptional for being noiseless.

The pistol was only four inches long and had a clip that held three bullets—a lead bullet to knock down the target, a steel one to kill, and a cyanide-tipped bullet for extremely close-range work. The cigarette cases were leather and hinged at the top. When opened, they appeared to hold only cigarettes, but inside were .32-caliber barrels that could be fired by pressing on the metal bars beside each barrel—a persuasive incentive to quit smoking.

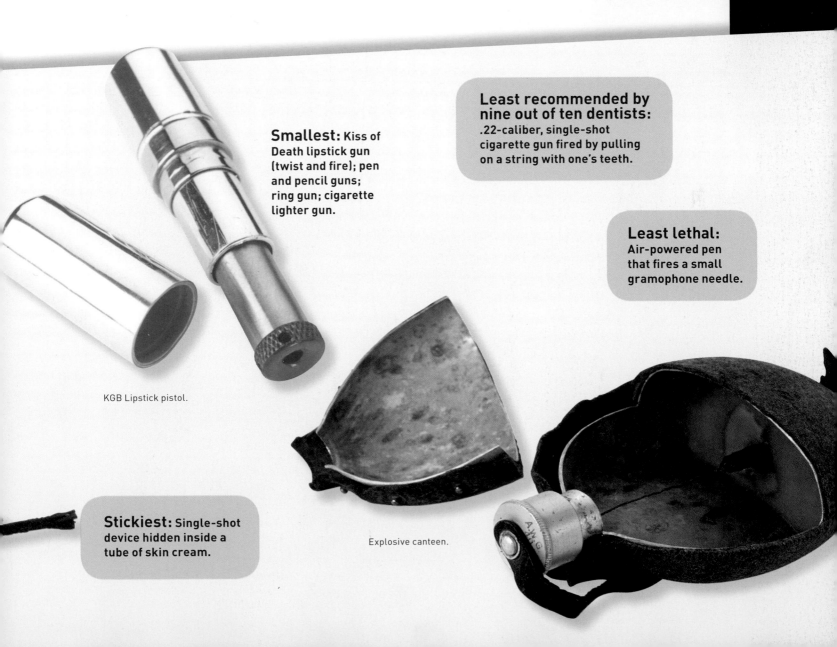

Smallest: Kiss of Death lipstick gun (twist and fire); pen and pencil guns; ring gun; cigarette lighter gun.

Least recommended by nine out of ten dentists: .22-caliber, single-shot cigarette gun fired by pulling on a string with one's teeth.

Least lethal: Air-powered pen that fires a small gramophone needle.

KGB Lipstick pistol.

Stickiest: Single-shot device hidden inside a tube of skin cream.

Explosive canteen.

15.

As dead drop sites go, Martha Peterson's was pleasantly scenic, though hardly covert—a heavily traveled bridge above the Moscow River within sight of Luzhniki sports stadium. There was nothing extraordinary in a thirty-three-year-old woman pausing to enjoy the view, at least not until she casually placed a rock under the bridge railing . . . and disappeared.

Peterson, an American embassy official and CIA officer had fallen into a trap set by the KGB that day in 1977. The floor beneath her feet literally opened up, and she dropped to a platform just below, where the Soviet agents were waiting. Those same agents had earlier nabbed Peterson's Soviet asset at the same spot. Although Peterson claimed it was a mistake, the evidence inside the hollow rock she'd used as a dead drop was not supportive of her assertion: a camera, money, a microphone, a phrase book, and, according to a story in the government controlled newspaper *Izvestia*, two poison capsules intended for a Soviet target of the CIA. Peterson was expelled the next day.

Peterson's capture, while dramatic, was hardly unique. Getting caught is an occupational hazard for spies—and often a fatal one. (Those cyanide capsules supplied to secret agents in Hollywood movies are not an imaginative invention. Though rarely used, they are available in case of capture.) Sometimes it's the agent's fault, a result of sloppy tradecraft or an indiscreet conversation. More often, however, agents are caught because someone, a defector or another captured agent, betrays them.

During World War II, for example, German agents dismantled a massive Russian espionage ring in their country after finding three men operating a clandestine radio. Under torture those Russian agents revealed enough of the Red Orchestra spy network to lead to the capture and execution of hundreds of the mostly German members of the ring.

Even the best agents make mistakes. Russian spymaster Rudolf Abel was arrested in New York City in 1957 after accidentally paying a newspaper boy with a hollow nickel. The junior G-man immediately took the nickel and his suspicions to the FBI, which found enough incriminating evidence in Abel's apartment to have him convicted and sentenced to thirty years in prison.

The one American in this anti-Nazi operation was Mildred Fish of Wisconsin. Her last words before her beheading were, "And I have loved Germany so much."

Despite his one mistake, Abel was so skilled at his craft that after his capture, CIA director Allen Dulles said, "I wish we had a couple like him in Moscow."

"What took you so long?"—FBI special agent Robert Hanssen to his captures on the occasion of his arrest.

Martha Peterson after being caught on the bridge.

Powers was sentenced to two years in prison but was exchanged for Soviet spy Rudolf Abel, the agent fingered by the newspaper boy. Powers quit the CIA and became a traffic reporter in Los Angeles. He died in a helicopter crash while reporting in 1977.

Photos of Gary Powers and his crashed U-2 taken by his Soviet captors.

nouncing America for spying. The United States, assuming that Powers had been killed in the crash, said the plane was engaged in "upper air studies," and if it had strayed into Soviet airspace, it was likely because the pilot had passed out.

Five days after the downing, Khrushchev played his ace by announcing that Powers was "alive and kicking." President Eisenhower had no choice but to admit the deception. One piece of collateral damage was the USSR's withdrawal from a summit meeting in Paris that same month and cancellation of a visit to Moscow by Eisenhower.

George Blake, the British intelligence mole who tipped his Russian handlers to the Berlin tunnel, was betrayed by a Polish defector in 1961. He admitted his guilt, claiming to have exposed four hundred British-controlled agents, and was sentenced to forty-two years in prison. In the spy business, his exposure followed a well-worn plot line.

What made George Blake so unusual was not his capture but his eventual escape. At Wormwood Scrubs Prison in London, Blake was befriended by Sean Bourke, a member of the Irish Republican Army, and two anti-nuclear-weapons activists. After those friends were released, they organized (most likely with help from the KGB) his escape.

Blake removed an iron bar in his cell he'd already loosened, lowered himself to a roof, and dropped four feet to the ground. At the prison wall he climbed a rope ladder that Bourke had provided and then jumped the last twenty feet to freedom.

After the drop knocked him unconscious and broke his wrist, his friends had to carry Blake to the car. A few weeks later he was given a hero's welcome in Moscow.

Spy Catchers

She'd had a great career with the CIA—case officer and field operative, and the first woman to run an intelligence station in Africa. But as she faced mandatory retirement in 1991, Jeanne Vertefeuille couldn't bear to think she might have let a traitor get away.

We'd had a sudden and unexplained loss of assets [agents] in 1985. We called them the Crown Jewels and we lost them all. Arrested, put on trial and with few exceptions executed. I was convinced we had a mole.

Vertefeuille persuaded her boss to let her spend her final eighteen months at the agency reexamining the six-year-old evidence. At the same time, another female CIA officer with twenty-plus years, Sandy Grimes, was on the verge of retiring when one of her superiors asked if she'd like

Bourke claimed he had to borrow more than $1,000 to free Blake. After a short trip to the Soviet Union, he returned to Ireland and wrote a book, *The Springing of George Blake*. The Irish government refused British requests to extradite him. Before he died (at age forty-seven), Bourke said, "I have never been a Communist . . . I sprang Blake from a slow, lingering death."

to join Vertefeuille in resurrecting the mole hunt. She said she'd even do it for free.

This fortuitous partnership, along with the work of two FBI special agents, led to the arrest in 1994 of Aldrich Ames, the most damaging mole in CIA history. Ames began spying for the USSR in 1985 while in the CIA's Directorate of Operations—Soviet and Eastern European Division. He was promised more than $2 million for betraying a number of Soviet intelligence officers who were secretly cooperating with the CIA, at least ten of whom were executed. In addition, he compromised 100 or so other covert operators in the Soviet Union and East Europe. The story of his capture illustrates how much of intelligence work depends on individual initiative.

Ames was no stranger to either woman. In fact, Sandy Grimes had carpooled with him in the early 1970s. "You'd have loved him," she told an audience at the International Spy Museum, where she and Vertefeuille lectured on the Ames case in spring 2004. "Back then he was an absentminded professor, always running out of his house late with his shirt out, saying, 'Sorry, sorry, sorry.'"

Aldrich Ames being handcuffed during his arrest.

Ames's first overture to the Soviet Union occurred in 1985, when he walked through the front door of its embassy in Washington, DC, and presented staff with information on three active cases and a letter requesting $50,000. Ames made the move because of financial problems brought on by a divorce and a new wife with expensive tastes. Within a few months Ames was carrying a shopping bag filled with classified documents out of CIA headquarters, to swap for money at a Georgetown watering hole.

"I liked him too," admitted Vertefeuille, who looks more like a kindly, gray-haired aunt than a seasoned ops officer. "He was a good storyteller, an erudite guy. If you told me he would be the worst mole in CIA history, I'd have bet you a million dollars."

Ames was transferred to Italy in 1986, distancing him from contact with information that would compromise agents. Coincidentally, at the same time, stricter procedures were instituted at CIA Headquarters and so the loss of assets stopped and the investigation was put on hold. However, Ames was still spying and still being paid. Vertefeuille noted:

> Before he went to Rome there was never any sign of affluence. He drove a twelve-year-old Volvo, lived in a rented apartment, had bad teeth, and looked like he cut his own hair. When he comes back we're flabbergasted. I swear he's wearing $500 Italian shoes and magnificent suits. His fingernails are manicured. His hair all done and his teeth fixed. He'd always slumped over before, but now he stood very erect, very proud, very arrogant.

The wealth went far beyond personal grooming. He bought a house for $540,000, paying in cash. He drove a $40,000 Jaguar. Alarm bells did go off in the agency, but Ames had a workable excuse—his second wife, Rosario, came from a fabulously wealthy family in South America.

When the investigation resumed in 1991, Ames was among twenty-five people on the active list. He'd already passed one lie-detector test in 1986, and now he passed another. But his answer to an impromptu quiz aroused suspicions. Said Vertefeuille:

> We asked, "If you were going to approach the KGB [Russian intelligence] how would you do it?" Agents love role-playing but when we asked Rick, he didn't do very well and that was not like him.

Vertefeuille programmed a computer ("This was the first computer investigation in the history of the agency," she said) to look at forty-six fields connecting all the operations and compromised agents to anyone working for the CIA or FBI. Sandy Grimes compiled a logbook of every move Ames made at the agency, arranged in chronological order, showing arrivals, departures, meetings, and meals he had had on company time. One of the CIA officers, Dan Payne, retrieved 560 pages of Ames's financial receipts, from bank statements and credit card bills to business expenses.

What Grimes called the "Eureka moment" occurred when Payne handed her a piece of paper showing a deposit of $8,500 to a bank the day after

When the CIA sent an agent to check it out, he returned with a report verifying Ames's story. Unfortunately, the agent had investigated the wrong part of her family tree. Rosario's branch was relatively bare.

Ames met with his authorized Soviet contact. They found the same pattern in a meeting two weeks later. When the day after the next meeting showed no deposit, the team was disappointed—but only until Payne came back to say it had been a federal holiday. And there, one day later, was another deposit of cash.

They were granted permission to tap Ames's phones and secretly enter his house to install cameras and electronic bugs on his computers and telephones. The night before every trash pickup, agents took his cans to a warehouse and studied each item before putting it all back.

"That was a nasty job," recalled Vertefeuille. "They had a five-year-old child who wasn't potty trained."

They sprang the trap on Ames the day before he was to go to the Soviet Union to a conference on narcotics. He was given a life sentence without parole. His wife was sentenced to sixty-four months.

"He was utterly and totally surprised," said Vertefeuille. "He was so cocky, he thought, *These dumb broads, they'll never catch me.*"

"He was wrong," added Grimes.

16.

British front-line observer leaping for life from his disabled balloon.

SPIES IN THE SKY

The U-2 was the perfect spy plane, a turbojet glider with a four-thousand-mile range and the most impressive camera ever invented—seven apertures recording simultaneously from high above the clouds. What set the spy plane on top of the espionage heap was its ability to take high resolution photographs (a tennis ball on a parking lot) from ninety thousand feet, safely above the kill range of any attack jet or missile.

The U-2 was fast, elegant, perfect—until it was downed by a Soviet missile. It apparently had one small glitch: an occasional stall in thin atmosphere that required it to glide lower before reignition. And that's where the Soviet missile was waiting.

The 1960 downing of Gary Powers's U-2 spy plane was a turning point in the evolution of aerial espionage. That same year, the first successful U.S. photographic reconnaissance satellite was launched, and with it the direction of intelligence immediately shifted from manned spy planes to satellites.

The technical superiority of satellites was demonstrated by that first successful overflight of the Soviet Union. A Corona satellite photographed 1.6 million square miles of Soviet territory, more than all fourteen of the U-2 manned flights combined. A secondary benefit, and by no means a minor one, was that with satellites there was no worry about political fallout if a pilot was killed or captured during the operation.

The first agents who climbed trees or towers to get a better look at the enemy had been easy targets for snipers. Hot-air balloons were a successful attempt to keep them out of harm's way, but only until weapon makers extended their range.

The Soviets launched the world's first satellite, _Sputnik 1_, and the first long-range intercontinental ballistic missile in 1957. The United States, caught by surprise, immediately ramped up its own efforts in both areas.

"Thou wilt not trust
the air with secrets."
—Christopher Marlowe

German observer using a camera from the basket of a hot air balloon.

The invention of the airplane brought an immediate and dramatic change in aerial espionage. In the first month of World War I, British pilots successfully warned their ground troops in Belgium of a German advance, allowing those troops to escape. Within two years, the French were erecting film-development tents beside battlefields so that aerial photographs could be seen within an hour.

Aerial intelligence had become crucial to military strategy by World War II. In preparation for D-Day, the Allies took eighty-five thousand aerial photographs per day. The German Luftwaffe had its own aerial reconnaissance, but the accuracy and resolution of its camera equipment were less sophisticated.

Planes continued to play a role in aerial spying despite the ascendancy of satellites. One of the more dangerous assignments was for those pilots who gathered information on a rival's defense systems, radar, and response times by intentionally flying across restricted airspace. The information gained came at a cost in equipment and lives.

During America's Civil War, telegraph lines were strung five hundred feet from the Union army's hydrogen gas balloons to the ground. The Confederate army made do with inferior hot-air balloons and flag signals, but the outer skin of its balloons was more precious—silk dresses volunteered by the ladies of the Confederacy. After the invention of the airplane, unmanned balloons and kites were used experimentally and with little success to carry spy cameras over the Soviet Union and China until the late 1950s.

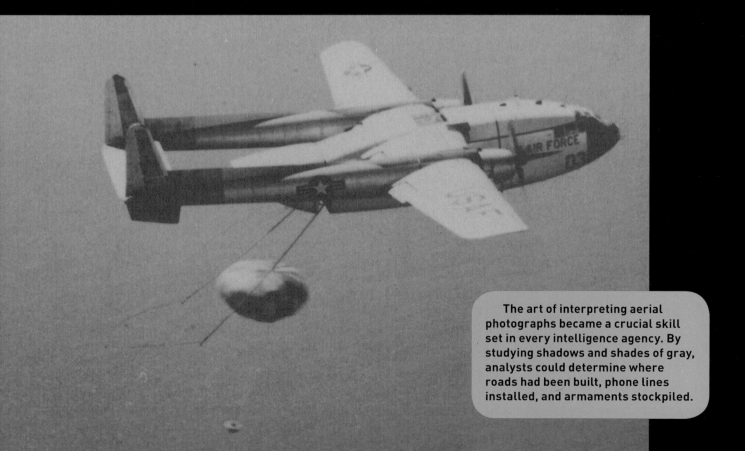

The art of interpreting aerial photographs became a crucial skill set in every intelligence agency. By studying shadows and shades of gray, analysts could determine where roads had been built, phone lines installed, and armaments stockpiled.

During the Cuban missile crisis, President Kennedy was able to convince skeptical European allies that the Soviets intended to deploy nuclear weapons in Cuba by showing aerial photographs of the missile containers. That evidence brought America allies for its blockade.

In the decades since, satellites have been used to collect critical information above Libya, Iran, Iraq, Nicaragua, Afghanistan, and Argentina (Falkland Islands)—areas where a downed espionage agent would have exacerbated tensions.

Satellite technology brought with it a new generation of analysts, spies, and traitors. In the 1970s Americans Andrew Lee and Christopher Boyce sold intelligence that helped block the satellite's reach to the Soviets. Boyce, who worked for high-tech satellite contractor TRW, recruited his friend Lee to transport documents to Soviet agents in Mexico City. Lee was caught there by Mexican police, who saw him throw a pouch onto the grounds of the Soviet embassy. A search of Lee found an envelope containing film of documents marked TOP SECRET.

The greatest benefit of satellite snooping was the lowering of international tension. Anxiety was reduced when nations could see, rather than guess at, a rival's military strength and feel somewhat confident that they would receive prior warning of missile firings. U.S. president Lyndon Johnson referred to this benefit in 1967 after satellites photographed the entire Soviet Union:

> Tonight we know how many missiles the enemy has and, it turned out, our guesses were way off. We were doing things we didn't need to do. We were building things we didn't need to build. We were harboring fears we didn't need to harbor.

The anti-ballistic-missile treaties negotiated between the United States and the Soviet Union were feasible only because of satellite verification. Below are some of the satellites designed for specific intelligence gathering:

- MIDAS: Used to detect Russian missile flame exhausts.
- RORSAT: Used to detect first Soviet ocean reconnaissance satellite.
- VELA: Used to detect nuclear explosions.
- RHYALITE: Used for telemetry gathering and signal intelligence.
- JUMPSEAT: Used for locating radar facilities.
- GAMBIT: Used to identify Soviet intercontinental missile deployments.
- SPOT: French, the first satellite available for commercial use.
- BIG BIRD: Used for low-altitude intelligence gathering.
- KENNAN: One of first satellites to transmit information digitally rather than by parachuting film buckets to be snagged by interceptor planes.

In 1958 a U.S. spy plane with seventeen on board was downed by Soviet MiG fighters over Russian territory. The Soviets denied that their pilots had downed the plane, but the United States had intercepted voice conversation among the four Soviet pilots confirming it. The United States played those tapes at a UN Security Council meeting. Two years later the Soviets would retaliate, exposing the lie told by President Eisenhower by producing Gary Powers.

Satellite systems were so successful in gathering data that they multiplied the age-old problem of information overload: How to effectively search and interpret millions of photographs covering hundreds of thousands of miles? One strategy was to look for shortcuts. Because the Soviets tended to enclose missile sites within three fences, and the missile-carrying trailers could not make sharp turns, analysts programmed "three-fence installations" and "wide-turn roads" into photo scans.

Submerged

What balloons, airplanes, and espionage satellites accomplished from the sky, espionage submarines attempted to do on a smaller scale underwater. The earliest espionage work was the delivery of agents into tightly guarded areas, or a quick periscope view of an area inaccessible to surface ships. But with the development of nuclear-powered submarines in the 1950s, the underwater operations became more ambitious.

Another underwater espionage operation was outlined in the 1998 book *Blind Man's Bluff: The Untold Story of American Submarine Espionage*. It involved tapping Soviet undersea phone lines by utilizing deep submersible vehicles launched from submarines. These craft were also used to retrieve Soviet missile parts and other equipment that submarine cameras had identified on the ocean floor.

The most ambitious of the attempted retrievals involved an entire Soviet submarine, the *Golf II*, which had sunk in the Pacific Ocean. The United States spent $500 million in the failed attempt. The only section raised contained a water-soaked diary and the remains of six crew members. They were buried at sea, and a videotape of the ceremony was given to the Soviet Union years later at the end of the Cold War by Director of Central Intelligence Robert Gates.

> **Operation HOLYSTONE** was a U.S. effort to identify and track all Soviet submarines. By following closely in the Soviet submarine's wake, the U.S. submarine was able to block its own sound. According to a story in *The New York Times*, the purpose of the operation was to identify the location of all Soviet submarines to quickly destroy them in the event of nuclear war.

> During World War I spy cameras were strapped to the chests of birds in the hope of getting valuable aerial photographs. The results were, unsurprisingly, a disappointment, since the birds moved erratically. But birds have been successfully used for centuries to carry messages during wartime. The pluckiest of these winged agents might have been Black Check Cock, a carrier pigeon with his own code name, CHER AMI. His last mission was a flight during World War I to notify U.S. Army intelligence that a battalion led by a Major Whittlesey was starving and under fire from enemy machine guns. CHER AMI flew twenty-five miles in twenty-five minutes, arriving at headquarters badly damaged but with the message intact. The 194 men of the battalion were saved—but alas, CHER AMI succumbed to his injuries. He was awarded the French Croix de Guerre with Palm for his heroic action, the only animal ever presented that award.

17.

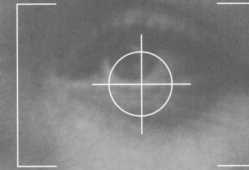

CELEBRITY SPIES

Few spymasters would have picked Josephine Baker for espionage work. In 1939 the American-born star of the Folies-Bergére theater in Paris was one of Europe's most popular entertainers, celebrated for her beauty, sensual dancing, and wit. (In one routine she danced in a skirt made of bananas, escorted on stage by a leopard.) That fame and the fact that she was a black woman living in an overwhelmingly white country would have argued against Baker doing anything undercover.

But after France declared war on Germany in 1939, the chief of military counterintelligence in Paris recruited her as an informer. Baker was eager to spy for her adopted country, and she played the role as well as any she'd performed on stage.

While celebrity inevitably shines too brightly for agents who work in the shadows, there are occasions when it can be advantageous. Josephine Baker, for example, was successful because she exploited her celebrity rather than trying to disguise it. She developed friendships with Italian and Japanese embassy officials in Paris, who were thrilled to talk to her about anything—love, jazz, German troop placements.

On the two occasions when Baker smuggled important documents into and out of France, she took the precaution of hiding some in her clothing and concealing others on sheet music with invisible ink. She needn't have bothered: Customs agents let her pass as though she were royalty. At the end of the war, Baker was awarded the Croix de Guerre and Medal of Resistance.

Another celebrity who used his renown as an espionage tool was British novelist and playwright Somerset Maugham. In the years before World War I, Maugham had four plays running simultaneously in London. In 1915, just after the start of that war, his novel *Of Human Bondage* became a best seller. The head of Britain's MI6 intelligence service in France recognized his celebrity as an opportunity and recruited Maugham to act as his agent.

Josephine Baker's return to the United States in 1951 was less triumphant. When the former Broadway performer was refused service at New York City's Stork Club because of her color, she declared her own war against racism. By refusing to perform at any theater that wasn't integrated, she pressured some to change their admission policies.
In 1963 she was one of the speakers, along with Martin Luther King Jr., at the civil rights movement's March on Washington, DC.

"He can speak seven languages, but he can't hit in any of them."
—*Teammate of Moe Berg, major-league baseball catcher and spy*

British writer and playwright, Christopher Marlowe.

1585

OD ME NVTRIT
DESTRVIT

Another British writer,
playwright Christopher
Marlowe, whom some have
argued was the real author
of Shakespeare's plays,
worked as an agent for British
spymaster Francis Walsingham
in the sixteenth century. He
played a role in uncovering the
Babington Plot to assassinate
England's Queen Elizabeth I.
Marlowe's espionage career
ended when he was killed in
a pub knife fight.

Marlene Dietrich offered her services to J. Edgar Hoovor as a spy for the FBI during World War II.

Using his natural cover, Maugham was able to travel through Europe, Samoa, and Russia, asking questions that would have aroused suspicion coming from anyone but a writer. His manuscripts were the ideal vehicles for sending encrypted information to and from London.

Marlene Dietrich, the German singer and actress who became a U.S. citizen after Hitler assumed power in Germany, offered her services to J. Edgar Hoover as a spy for the FBI during World War II.

Dietrich entertained Allied troops at the front lines in Africa, Italy, France, and Germany, occasionally riding in General George Patton's jeep. She also worked with the U.S. Office of Strategic Services (OSS)—the forerunner of the CIA—to broadcast songs and messages to German troops, encouraging them to lay down their arms. It's not known whether she actually undertook any spy missions, but after the war she was honored by the United States, France, and Belgium.

Moe Berg was not your average major-league baseball player. A linguist and scholar, he studied philosophy at the Sorbonne and had degrees from Princeton and Columbia Law School. And what other professional athlete made home movies that were used in American bombing raids, or traveled to Switzerland with a license to kill?

Berg's first espionage coup came in 1934 while traveling in Japan with a major-league All-Star team. With a movie camera hidden under his kimono, Berg, who spoke Japanese, talked his way onto the roof of a Tokyo hotel to film the skyline and harbor. Eight years later General James Doolittle used this home movie to plan the first air raid on Tokyo.

During another overseas trip, Berg left his companions to sneak into Norway and confirm the location of a Nazi nuclear research facility. His most important assignment came in 1943, after he'd retired from baseball and was working for the OSS. He was sent to Zurich to hear a lecture by Werner Heisenberg, the head of Nazi Germany's atomic bomb project. Berger was tasked to listen to the lecture (he was fluent in German) and, if he determined Germany was close to developing a bomb, kill Heisenberg. While it may seem wildly improbable that someone without at least a degree in physics would be asked to make such an assessment, the story is true. As it happened, Berg kept the pistol in his pocket.

Daniel Defoe, the eighteenth-century author of *Robinson Crusoe* and *Moll Flanders*, has been called the father of British intelligence, less for his fieldwork than for his ideas about organizing that service. Defoe's first espionage assignment sent him to Scotland, where, he admits in his diary, he was foiled by the Scottish burr. "We could understand nothing on this side of what the people said, any more than if we had been in Morocco."

During Berg's fifteen-year major-league career as a catcher with five teams, including the Washington Senators, he had a batting average of only .243. But he was more of a hit performing undercover work.

Once, while traveling through Czechoslovakia with other OSS agents, Berg and his companions were challenged by Soviet troops to show authorization for being there. Berg unfolded a letter adorned with a giant red star, and they were allowed to pass. What Berg had shown them was a letter from the Texaco Oil Company, which still uses the red star as its corporate symbol.

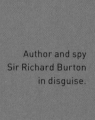

In India, Burton dyed his skin and worked in labor gangs. He later traveled as a peddler there to pick up intelligence about tribal factions and plots against the British rulers.

Author and spy
Sir Richard Burton
in disguise.

Sir Richard Burton (no relation to the renowned actor) didn't need to exploit his fame when he spied for England during the height of its colonial empire. The author and translator of the *Kama Sutra* and *Arabian Nights* was fluent in more than thirty languages and a master of disguise. During his travels on behalf of British intelligence in India, Africa, and much of the Middle East, Burton would disguise himself as a native and walk among the people.

Burton led intelligence expeditions in Somaliland and Abyssinia. In East Africa he searched for the source of the Nile. He was possibly the first Westerner to make a pilgrimage to the holy city of Mecca (disguised as a merchant and going by the name of Mizra Abdullah El Bushiri). No one else could have obtained the information he provided the British.

Julia Child would later become famous for her cooking shows, but in 1944 the thirty-one-year-old was issued a gas mask, canteen, and pith helmet by the OSS and shipped to China. "I was just a file clerk," she'd say later, but the files Child handled were explosive. She collected top-secret documents outlining an invasion of Malaysia and espionage in Southeast Asia. Though her co-workers recalled she was not much of a cook at that time, she did concoct a recipe that helped in the war effort. Sharks kept bumping into and blowing up underwater explosives designed to sink German U-boats. Child and some of her colleagues mixed up a shark repellent, which kept them at bay.

John Ford, who directed seventy-four films including the Oscar-winning *Grapes of Wrath*, won another Oscar and a Purple Heart for an eighteen-minute documentary titled *The Battle of Midway*.

Saul Steinberg, a Romanian cartoonist whose work appeared in *The New Yorker* magazine, became a U.S. citizen in 1943, joined the navy that same year, and was assigned to teach Chinese guerrillas how to destroy bridges with dynamite. His next assignment was more suited to his skills. The director of the OSS sent him to North Africa, where he drew cartoons for a resistance newspaper that was created by the OSS and dropped behind enemy lines.

Hollywood director John Ford headed the field photographic unit of the OSS.

Ford, the head of the OSS field photographic branch, was at Midway when Japanese planes attacked. While most of the marines went underground, the forty-year-old Ford volunteered to stay in a power plant with eight young marines serving as spotters. Ford took advantage of the position to film the attack, which he later described in an interview:

> I was close to the hangar and I was lined up on it with my camera, figuring it would be one of the first things they got. It wasn't any of the dive bombers [that got it]. A Zero flew about 50 feet over it and dropped a bomb and hit it, the whole thing went up. I was knocked unconscious. Just knocked me goofy for a bit, and I pulled myself out of it. I did manage to get the picture. . . . you can see one big chunk coming for the camera.
>
> The Marines with me . . . they were kids, oh, I would say from 18 to 22, none of them were older. They were the calmest people I have ever seen. They were up there popping away with rifles having a swell time and none of them were alarmed. I mean the thing [a Japanese bomb] would drop through, they would laugh and say "My God that one was close." I figured then, well, if these kids are American kids, I mean this war is practically won.

Another OSS operative during World War II was film actor Sterling Hayden (*The Godfather, Dr. Strangelove*). He left Hollywood to join the U.S. Marines, enlisting under the name John Hamilton to avoid publicity, then finagled a transfer to the OSS. Hayden, who'd sailed around the world by the time he was twenty, commanded ships in the Mediterranean that delivered guns and supplies to guerrillas in Yugoslavia fighting the Germans.

Hayden was later part of an OSS unit that pushed into Germany as that army retreated. He later talked about what he'd seen:

> There came squirming into the light millions of anti-Nazis. It was tough, they said, waving handkerchiefs and wringing their hands with joy, to have lived under Hitler. . . . The real anti-Nazis were dead or in exile, or in Belsen, Auschwitz, Buchenwald. Names we thought at the time that would teach us a lesson we'd never forget.

Hayden returned to Hollywood after the war with a Silver Star.

Actor Sterling Hayden, another OSS operative during World War II.

18.

THE CULTURE
OF SPIES

The Western world's earliest fictional spies were not overly burdened by charisma. Consider Harvey Birch, the harassed peddler in James Fenimore Cooper's 1821 novel *The Spy*, who was wrongly accused of selling information to the British when he was actually one of George Washington's secret agents. Or Joseph Conrad's incompetent shopkeeper and double agent Verloc, in the 1907 novel *The Secret Agent*, who plots with anarchists in his London basement to blow up the Greenwich Observatory but accomplishes only his own death by his wife's hand.

Of course those early agents did not have the confidence that high-tech gadgets provided later fictional spies—James Bond's lethal helicopter, hand delivered in red-velvet-lined suitcases, or Matt Helm's exploding coat buttons and backward-firing gun, to name a few. More to the point, spies at the beginning of the twentieth century were regarded by the public as sneaky and subversive.

But a hundred years later secret agents, especially in the world of popular entertainment, are the gold standard. Need dramatic tension in your best seller? Set Jack Ryan on the trail of international narco-terrorists. Sex appeal in your movie? Why not let British actress Elizabeth Hurley help Austin Powers get back his mojo from Dr. Evil. For family viewing, the latest release of *Spy Kids* is available at your local video store.

Covers of G-Men books, a popular post-World War I spy series along with other G-Men toys.

"This tape will self-destruct in five seconds."
—Introduction to TV's Mission: Impossible

The journey from low regard to public adulation got an early push from Britain's E. Phillips Oppenheimer. After the creation of England's Secret Service in 1909, he wrote a number of books about the expertise of British agents, particularly *Havoc* in 1910, which dealt with a secret alliance between Germany and Russia that England was bound to foil.

In the years after World War I, spy literature made a great leap sideways, becoming more optimistic, adventurous, and popular. In the United States this trend was personified by the pulp-fiction hero Jimmy Christopher—Secret Service Operator 5, a blond-haired, blue-eyed firebrand who "possessed a poise that added stature to his years and obviously he was American through and through." Operator 5 matched wits with the Melting Death, Master of Broken Men, and the War Dogs of the Green Destroyer with an array of weapons, including a rapier and a death's head ring that held a powerful explosive. In his posse were a manservant, a shoeshine boy, and a girlfriend who was forever being strapped to cannons, kegs of dynamite, and railroad tracks.

Radio shows adopted espionage themes as well. The most popular chronicled the exploits of Captain Midnight, who fought foreign sabotage with his small band of followers, including his mechanic Ichabod Mudd. Radio listeners could help the captain by sending him an Ovaltine label, which would earn them a Code-O-Graph to decipher important messages.

As World War II approached, serious writers began incorporating the growing threat of Fascism into their work. British author Eric Ambler wrote half a dozen novels between 1936 and 1940 warning of the trouble ahead, including *The Dark Frontier* and *Uncommon Danger*. Ambler's protagonists were often ordinary citizens who stumbled into espionage situations that required not only courage but also skills to match those of a trained nemesis.

The early movies of Alfred Hitchcock developed this same theme. His 1934 film *The Man Who Knew Too Much* centered on a protagonist whose son was kidnapped by the villainous foreigner Peter Lorre. Later, in his classic film *North by Northwest*, Cary Grant was mistaken for a government undercover agent by foreign spies.

The war also produced a bumper crop of spy authors, not all of them good. Malcolm Muggeridge, who was both a writer and an intelligence agent during the war, said that this army of unschooled writers took to espionage "as easily as the mentally unstable become psychiatrists."

The brutality of World War II and the Cold War that followed produced a more conflicted and brooding spy literature with anti-hero protagonists. Two excellent British writers, Graham Greene and John le Carré, exemplified this new sensibility. Greene's 1955 novel *The Quiet American* looked at the death and mayhem caused by an idealistic CIA agent in Vietnam during

Germany's Kaiser Wilhelm was known to be reluctant to go to war against England. The reason? After reading Oppenheimer's spy novels, he feared his own spy network would be no match for that of Britain.

The Soviet Union had its own surge of spy and crime pulp fiction immediately after the war. One of the more popular characters was Mike Thingmaster, whose secret organization of politically correct workers tried to "mend the mess" caused by Fascists and Capitalists. Millions of those pulp books were sold before the Communist party decreed them to be anti-Revolutionary.

World War II provided obvious story lines for filmmakers. *The Man Who Never Was* deals with a corpse dressed in a military uniform and fitted with fake documents, who helps deceive Germany about where Allied military forces plan to invade Italy. *The Iron Curtain* was about Soviet defector Igor Gouzenko, who brings information that implicates Soviet and American spies working in the United States, including members of the atomic spy ring who gave information on the atomic bomb to the Soviet Union.

Writer John leCarré captured the grim reality of spying during the Cold War.

Western spy authors Tom Clancy, Robert Ludlum, John le Carré, Ian Fleming, and Frederick Forsyth have each sold more than fifty million books. The Soviet Union's best-selling author, Julian Semyonov, at one time had thirty-five million books in print.

The Third Man (1949), based on a novel by Graham Greene, is considered by many to be the best British film ever made. Orson Welles plays Harry Lime, a character Greene modeled after Cambridge spy Kim Philby. But it is the setting of postwar Vienna that may be the film's true star, as much a threat as any of the flesh-and-blood villains. The film ends with a chase scene through Vienna's sewers, which one critic said "physically embody the moral cesspool that Cold War Europe was becoming."

the 1950s. Later novels explored the same theme in Cuba, Haiti, Panama, and other hot spots of the Cold War.

In John le Carré's novel *The Secret Pilgrim*, disillusioned spymaster George Smiley says, "We scarcely paused to ask ourselves how much longer we could defend our society by these means and remain a society worth defending." One of his best books, *The Spy Who Came In from the Cold*, ends with a British agent and a woman friend shot and killed at the base of the Berlin Wall.

But just as that existential darkness descended, there rose a new espionage warrior to light the way with a nuclear-powered flashlight provided by his gadget master Q (based on Charles Fraser-Smith, the inventor of World War I spy devices for the British government). When James Bond, British Secret Agent 007, jumped from the pages of Ian Fleming's fourteen novels onto movie screens in 1963 with *Dr. No* and *From Russia with Love*, the general public's perception of secret agents was forever changed. This Bond fellow romanced beautiful women, dressed impeccably, and dispatched evildoers without breaking a sweat.

Ian Fleming's best-selling novels were popular with American president John F. Kennedy and were required reading for Russian KGB agents (Fleming had been in British naval intelligence). But the Bond of these books was bulked up for the movies. In *Spy Book*, authors Norman Polmar and Thomas B. Allen note: "Bond, who could at times be believable in the pages of a book, was incredible on the screen. Stunts, gadgets, and hair-breadth escapes were the standard plot ingredients. Readers of the Bond books hardly recognized their hero when he went Hollywood."

The success of the Bond movies opened the door to a host of other spy films including *The Ipcress File* and *Funeral in Berlin*, based on the novels of Len Deighton, and *The Fourth Protocol* based on a Frederick Forsyth book. European filmmakers also jumped onto the bandwagon with some good, as well as campy films. In the 1966 Italian movie *Flashman*, a scientist develops a serum for invisibility and is killed by his assistant, who uses the serum to rob banks. Into the plot steps Flashman, a costumed hero with a British butler.

Television was quick to follow cinema's lead. The most popular of the TV spy shows was *Mission: Impossible*, with a cast that included a black technical wizard, a master of disguise, a sultry woman who flirted her way through closed doors, and Peter Graves, the brains of the outfit.

The Man from U.N.C.L.E., a forerunner of détente, starred American agent Napoleon Solo and his Russian partner Illya Kuryakin. The most stylish of the television shows was Britain's *The Avengers*, featuring

Opposite page: Robert Vaughn in *The Man from U.N.C.L.E.*

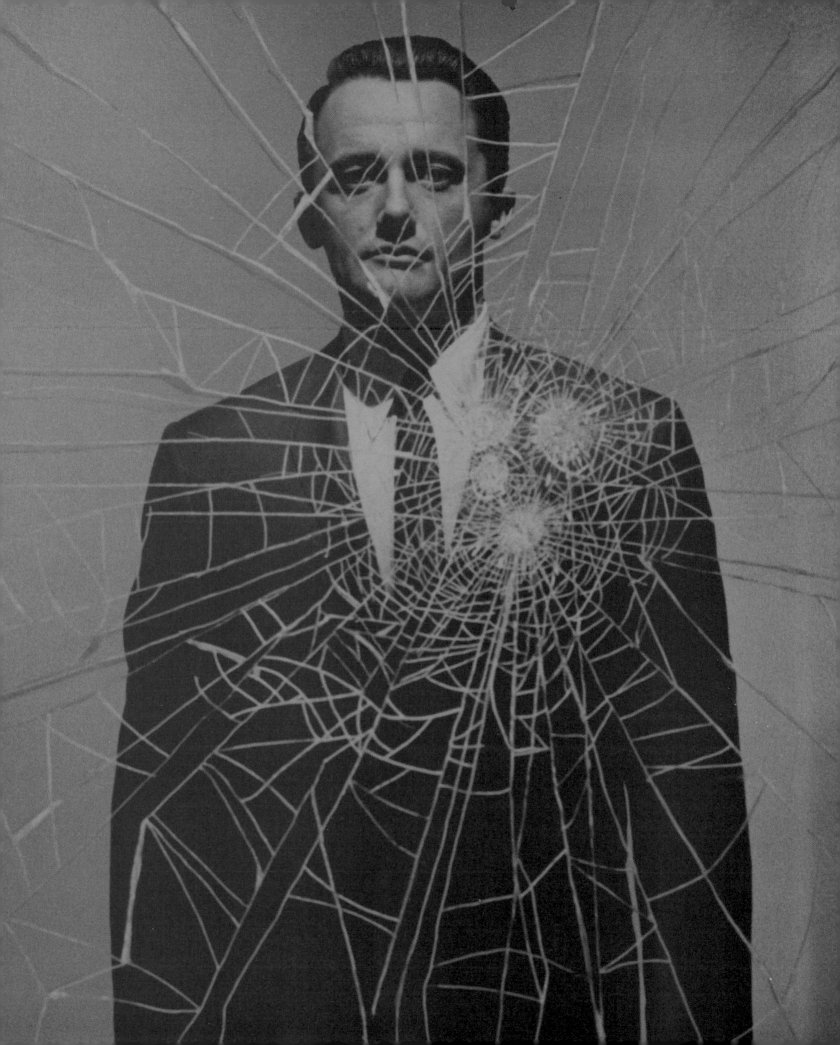

The villain in one episode of *Get Smart* was the Groovy Guru, who told his acolytes to make war not love and planned to poison the minds of America's youth with the songs of his band, the Sacred Cows.

Emma Peel (Diana Rigg) and John Steed (Patrick McNee) as a witty duo fighting their way through psychedelic England with furled umbrellas and the occasional karate chop.

Many of these television shows contained more than a hint of parody, but none was as ridiculously funny as *Get Smart*, which ran from 1965 to 1970. The cult show, which is a predecessor to the Austin Powers films, was written by Mel Brooks and Buck Henry (who also wrote the screenplay for *The Graduate*). A stew of bizarre characters, great dialogue, and silly sight gags, *Get Smart* poked fun at Bond films, *The Man from U.N.C.L.E.*, *Casablanca*, *The Maltese Falcon* . . . in short, just about everything.

The main characters were Agent 86, Maxwell Smart (Don Adams), a cowardly, egocentric, and ultimately likable klutz in constant need of rescue by his beautiful and talented assistant, Agent 99 (Barbara Feldman). The bad guys of KAOS, including Bronzefinger, Dr. Yes, and Rotten Rupert Rathskellar, tried turning them into wax statues and using sound waves to make their brains explode.

While James Bond's signature line was "Shaken not stirred," Maxwell Smart's was "Sorry about that, Chief." His best espionage tool was a shoe phone (forerunner to today's ubiquitous cell phone). Other gadgets, supplied to him by his Q equivalent, usually blew up in his own face. When Smart and the Chief needed a secure place to talk, they'd lower plastic Cones of Silence over their heads, which naturally made it impossible to hear one another.

In one of the messages Smart always delivered at the end of each show, he said to his assistant: "But 99, we have to destroy, shoot, and kill—we represent all that is wholesome and good in the world."

The KGB, upset at being bested at every turn by the fictional Bond, commissioned writer Julian Semyonov to create a Soviet agent to undermine the "cult of the decadent Western spy." In 1973 Russian television audiences got their own spy show based on Semyonov's work—*Seventeen Moments of Spring*—starring intelligence agent Maxim Isaev, code name: SITLITZ. Among his achievements, he exposed a World War II plot by England and the United States to make a separate peace with Germany and join forces in attacking Russia.

I Spy broke ground with television's first black lead, intelligence agent Bill Cosby posing as a trainer for professional tennis bum Robert Culp (an agent as well). The pair often helped third-world citizens stand up to the forces of oppression, which inspired the CIA to provide copies of the show to developing nations.

Right: memorabilia from the popular television show *Get Smart*; opposite page: Barbara Feldman as Agent 99 in *Get Smart*.

159

EPILOGUE

The September 11, 2001 attacks on the World Trade Center and Pentagon suggest parallels to the Japanese bombing of Pearl Harbor, which in 1941 represented the worst loss of American lives in a single day due to a foreign attack—until 9/11 surpassed it. In the aftermath of each, the country's intelligence services were criticized for failing to foresee the sneak attacks.

A national commission investigating September 11 did find fault with U.S. intelligence, concluding that at least some of the hijackers should have been detected either entering the country or going through airport security. Furthermore, intelligence agencies had been warned of the possible use of hijacked airplanes as weapons. As was the case at Pearl Harbor, the commission also found a lamentable reluctance by intelligence agencies to share intelligence.

In a broader context, it has been argued that some of the U.S. intelligence problems are due to its great success in gathering information. New and controversial projects—such as the National Security Agency's ECHELON, which is designed to intercept phone calls, e-mails, and microwave messages everywhere in the world, and the Pentagon's Total Information Awareness, which aims to collect personal data on everyone on the planet—create a near-infinite amount of intelligence for a decidedly finite number of analysts.

In 1968 former CIA officer Thomas W. Braden wrote in *The Washington Post* that the intelligence community "produces an amount of paper which God himself would have difficulty digesting even if He did not already know what the Russians were up to." And it would be generous to describe that volume as a pond compared to the information and data-rich ocean of today.

Not all of ECHELON's intelligence must be examined by analysts. After being collected at intercept stations around the world, the intelligence is put through National Security Agency computers, which use advanced filters to flag code words or phrases and alert analysts stationed at those sites. But the enormous volume of material can't help but diminish the perceived importance of any single piece.

As for Total Information Awareness—which, according to *The New York Times*, will give intelligence analysts and law enforcement officials instant access to "credit card and banking transactions and travel documents, without a search warrant"—the likely court battles and congressional hearings on privacy issues would surely affect its utility.

The one proposed program most likely to appear in an Austin Powers movie is called the Micromechanical Flying Insect—a fly spy. Scientists at a lab in Berkeley, California, have been given $2.5 million to study the aerodynamics of insects and hummingbirds and then build a mechanical fruit fly with all the speed and maneuverability of a real one. If it ever gets off the ground, the robofly would be equipped with video capability for flying above enemy troops, searching for chemical weapons, or, as some fear, spying on citizens.

However, intelligence observers worry that all the money and time devoted to TECHINT: technical intelligence (including the new generation of spy satellites due in 2005) hurts the effort to put more agents on the ground, HUMINT. One of the glaring weaknesses of American intelligence during the initial occupation of Iraq was the inability to infiltrate terrorist organizations because agents didn't have either the language skills or the correct ethnicity. The FBI had increased the number of counterterrorism agents from five hundred to seven thousand by 2003, but fewer than two dozen spoke Arabic.

There are those who advocate a return to first principles in the spy business, an emulation of spy operations such as that commissioned by sixteenth-century Mogul ruler Akbar, who deployed four thousand agents to walk his kingdom each day. Since the new army of terrorists does not have a nation to defeat or borders to invade, collecting intelligence may require this kind of patience and commitment.

To find the perfect spy for today's espionage needs, look to Rudyard Kipling's 1901 novel *Kim*. An Irish orphan raised as a Hindu by a poor, half-caste woman in India, Kim is able to assume the identity of a Hindu, a European, or a Muslim as he travels throughout India in clever disguises to spy for the British. Those disguises work because he not only looks the part but also knows the languages, habits, taboos, and spirit of the people with whom he associates.

For every satellite or robofly, it wouldn't hurt to have a dozen Kims on the spy roster as well. As former director of the CIA James Woolsey has stated, the breakup of the Soviet Union created a new world order, and with it a pressing need for new intelligence strategies.

SELECTED BIBLIOGRAPHY

Andrew, Christopher. Her Majesty's Secret Service: The Making of the British Intelligence Community. New York: Viking, 1986.

_____.For the President's Eyes Only: Secret Intelligence and the American Presidency from Washington to Bush. New York: HarperCollins, 1995.

Andrew, Christopher and Vasili Mitrokhin. The Sword and the Shield: The Mitrokhin Archive and the Secret History of the KGB. New York: Basic Books, 1999.

Dulles, Allen W. Great True Spy Stories. New York: Ballantine Books, 1968.

_____. The Craft of Intelligence. New York: Harper and Row, 1965.

Haynes, John E. Venona: Decoding Soviet Espionage in America. New Haven, Connecticut.: Yale University Press, 2000.

Hitz, Frederick P. The Great Game: The Myth and Reality of Espionage. New York: Alfred A. Knopf, 2004.

Kahn, David. The Codebreakers. New York: Signet, 1973.

Knightley, Phillip. The Second Oldest Profession: Spies and Spying in the Twentieth Century. New York: Norton, 1987.

O'Toole, G.J.A. Honorable Treachery. New York: Atlantic Monthly Press, 1991.

Polmar, Norman, and Thomas B Allen, Spy Book: The Encyclopedia of Espionage. New York: Random House, Inc., 1997.

Richelson, Jeffrey T., A Century of Spies: Intelligence in the Twentieth Century: New York: Oxford University Press, 1995.

Singh, Simon. The Code Book: The Science of Secrecy From Ancient Egypt to Quantum Cryptography. New York: Doubleday, 1999.

Volkman, Ernest, and Blaine Baggett. Secret Intelligence: The Inside Story of America's Espionage Empire. New York: Berkley Books, 1991.

PHOTO CREDITS

AFP Photo pg. 156

AP/Wide World Photos, pg. 50, 52, 64, 80, 95 (lower left) 104, 112, 117, 151

Bettmann/CORBIS pg. 9, 91,103, 114, 123

Bletchley Park Trust/Science & Society Picture Library pg. 79

CORBIS pg. ii, 1, 5

David Wise, *Nightmover: How Aldrich Ames Sold the CIA to the KGB for $4.6 Million* pg. 132

Dunlop Archive Project, London pg. 72

Es Geschah an Der Mauer by Rainer Hildebrandt. Berlin: Arbeitsgemeinschaft 13, 1977 pg. 116

Everett Collection/Courtesy Turner Entertainment Co.

Former Member of Bletchley pg. 78

Getty Images/Hulton Archive pg. 10, 26, 28 (lower right), 33, 60, 138

Getty Images/Popperfoto pg. 107

Greg Schaler/PhotoAssist/National Security Agency pg. 37

Hulton-Deutsch Collection/CORBIS pg. 146

Imperial War Museum, London pg. 17, 73

International Spy Museum, Washington, DC pg. 2, 4, 13, 24, 25, 28, 29, 36, 40, 41, 44, 51, 95 (lower right), 120, 124-5, 128, 130, 154

Jeffrey L. Rotman/CORBIS pg. 5

KEYSTONE Pressedienst GmbH & Co KG pg. 116

Library of Congress pg. 21, 61, 137

Luis Jimenez pg. 45

National Archives pg. 34, 73, 86, 139, 149

National Gallery, London, UK/Bridgeman Art Library pg. 8

National Trust/Art Resource, NY pg. 8

The Philby Files:The Secret Life of Master Spy Kim Philby **by Genrikh Borovik. New York: Little, Brown and Company, 1994** pg. 95 (upper right)

Picture Library, National Portrait Gallery, London, pg. 79, 148

Public Record Office pg. 75, 76

Smithsonian Institution, pg. 77

Retna, Ltd. pg. 87

Scott Bruce pg. 159

Underwood & Underwood/CORBIS pg. 47

William L. Clements Library, University of Michigan pg. 62, 63

SV - Bilderdienst pg. 113

INDEX